The Music of Consciousness

A NOVEL POEM

BY
EAMONN A O'SULLIVAN

STEDALT,
STAMULLEN,
CO MEATH.

authorHOUSE®

AuthorHouse™ UK
1663 Liberty Drive
Bloomington, IN 47403 USA
www.authorhouse.co.uk
Phone: 0800.197.4150

Published by AuthorHouse 12/19/2018

ISBN: 978-1-7283-8277-7 (sc)
ISBN: 978-1-7283-8284-5 (e)

Print information available on the last page.

Any people depicted in stock imagery provided by Getty Images are models, and such images are being used for illustrative purposes only. Certain stock imagery © *Getty Images.*

This book is printed on acid-free paper.

Contents

Chapter One

The Big Bang, Out Of A Singularity

"Standing on a well-chilled cinder, we see the slow fading of the suns and we try
to recall the vanished brilliance of the origin of the worlds..."
Georges Lemaitre

"The next time you complain that there is nothing on in any television channel,
remember that you can always watch the dancing static, that is, the birth of the universe."
Bill Bryson

1

In the beginning was the quantum dot.
What it was and whence it came we know not.
How All-There-Is could evolve and grow
From this nothing place, we do not know,
Thirteen point seven billion years ago,
But we gather, using mathematicals,

That a blizzard of subatomicals
Splashed and spluttered, flake on flake,
Along Time's inexorable wake,
Out of a singularity.

2

The "Big Bang" is the inelegant designation
For the sublime moment of Creation.
How could those two little words, so terse,
Carry the weight of the Universe?
An unthinkable mystery arrived
Laced with the languages of Life.
The who, the what, the why, the where,
If and whether and when were there
In an unanswerable questionnaire,
Inside the singularity.

3

This present that had no past that we know,
On the morning that had no yesterday,
That set the fireball on its way,
When all Existence was set free,
All-That-Would-Be, each possibility,
Out of the shadows into the light,
The gift of Now on its future way,
The sacramental actuality,
Spiritus Mundi, all we can see, not see,
Out of a singularity.

4

All-There-Was, All-There-Could-Be coalesced
In One, Unified, indefinable Whole,
Whose interconnected possibilities
Were locked inside impenetrabilities

Waiting to give the universe its soul,
And the sleeping seeds of Consciousness
Would wake incredible, illimitable,
Embryonic Resonances
As All-There-Is began its slow reveal
Out of that singularity.

5

Fields, magnetism, electricity,
Weak and strong nuclear forces, gravity,
Matter, every generic form of energy,
Light, alive, beyond space and time,
And the all-pervading Consciousness,
All intertwined in equivalence,
All interlaced in pure coherence,
All-That-Could-and-Would-Be
Was One and interchangeable,
Inside that singularity.

6

All began, indivisible and self-aware,
Like some telepathic reverie,
As all of Creation, sacred and alive,
All Creation, positively unified,
All-There-Could-be inborn creatively
In Conscious, knowing symmetry,
Everything striving in its Longing-To-Be
Stretching potential long fingers for
The Being-It-Could-Become
Out of that singularity.

7

In that moment out of Consciousness,
Infinite, eternal, spaceless, timeless,

A vast ocean of power and peace
With subtle ripples was released,
Enfolded and unfolding in a continuous
Spectrum of changing hierarchies
From then up to the eternal Now.
An awakening of the soul in its growing
Through the reality of its own knowing
All from that singularity.

8

From Consciousness sprung this issue,
Which, enfolded inside that quantum place
Would grow into an infinite sea
Of potential matter, energy and space
As it suddenly began to unfold and create
The universe in its evolving state
Out of the quantum dot, the Big Bang,
As a conker buried evolves to be
A great, great-rooted chestnut tree,
All from that singularity.

9

The Universe is drama on a cosmic stage.
Energy and matter are the strolling players.
Exits, entrances, written in scripts
By the laws of natural science-physics
In the secretive vaults of mathematics.
We must figure the complex storyline,
For thirteen point seven billion years,
Where we are going, where we have been,
After the stunning opening scene,
The marvellous singularity.

10

The first moments of Creation,
Moments of sudden, gigantic inflation,
Imprinted with genes of sky and sea,
A quantum universality,
A Stream-of-Consciousness set free,
From which would crawl the history
Of water, earth, air and fire,
Of fish, flesh, fowl and tree,
Of comic, tragic humanity,
Out of that singularity.

11

Ours, an ineffable reality,
Behind curtains of perplexity,
A puzzling, quizzical mystery,
Inside an enigma, a paradox, a fable,
And for all we think we know, unknowable.
Even creative imaginations
Have definitive limitations
About the nature of the dot,
Such as it was, what it was not,
Born in that singularity.

12

In the Big Bang we stare at the face
Of Creation, a nothing-to-everything place,
Knowing it happened in no place
And grew at once in every space
Into a universe so finely tuned
To a critical gravity in all of space
With a mathematical equipoise
Drawn to the fiftieth decimal place!

A difference of one and no human race
Could rise from that singularity!

13

From this bursting, cosmic, lightning flash,
Nervously jiggling a quantum dance,
Rose a beginning filled with quantum shiver,
Riven with indeterminacy,
A stencil to guide the Artist's brush
Which coloured in the drama's backdrop.
Space just suddenly appeared,
And Time ballooned out of nowhere
Both uneasy about being cramped
Inside that singularity.

14

We can conceive of anything everywhere
But not of nothing—it is nowhere.
Though born where only nothingness could be,
We live in the midst of eternity.
All else around, no entropy there,
Something was simply everywhere,
Nothing, strange as it seems, nowhere.
It happened here and only here
And grew around this little sphere,
The inexpressible singularity.

15

The actuality of invariable reality
Cannot be said to be fixed
Until observation proves it exists
And this implies a Consciousness.
This leaves us with the paradox:
Consciousness it seems relies on matter

And matter originates from Consciousness
Out of the aeons when nothing happened
To milliseconds when aeons happened
Inside that singularity?

16

Quantum physicists try to make sense
With exquisite mathematical elegance
Of the workings of the universe,
The way our little world goes around
Because of little particles that abound
And their Big Bang Theory portrays
Beginnings, billions of years ago, better
Than meteorologists today
Can predict tomorrow's weather,
Sprung from a singularity.

17

From this place of near infinite density,
Grew billions, billions of galaxies,
Each with billions, billions of entities,
Stars, moons, supernovae,
Suns, planets, nebulae,
Hammered out in the cosmic smithies,
Made from zillions of molecules,
The infinitesimal building blocks,
Matter's visible invisibilities,
All from that singularity.

18

Galaxies, billions of light years apart,
Awesome energy churning there,
Ineffable, turbulent atmosphere,
Far and beyond our imaginings,

From the holy grail of cosmology,
The moment its evolution would start,
A Conscious Power deep in the heart
Of our universe, our planet, our history,
Out of the inexpressible mystery
Of the ineffable singularity.

19

Truth lies in perfect simplicity.
Simplicity grew to complexity,
Complexity to incomprehensibility,
Incomprehensibility to mystery,
Mystery that veered towards near infinity.
Something, somehow, lit the spark
Of galaxies, black holes, molecules, quarks.
Something, somehow, switched the light
And all existence took to flight
Out of that singularity.

20

One way or another there had to be One
With the key to turn the ignition on.
Tell me which one is the greater?
Creation or this incredible Creator?
A simple question of intent
Where the answer is self-evident.
From this awesome womb was given birth
The beautiful, matchless, Planet Earth,
Alive with luminous Consciousness,
Born from the singularity.

21

Look here! Look there! The limitless,
Inimitable Consciousnesses

Of shimmering clouds of bluenesses,
The forty shades of greennesses,
The ambrosial scents of fragrances,
The honeyed tastes of sweetnesses,
The tingling thrill of sensuousness,
The tactile feel of smoothnesses,
The luminous flushes of brightnesses
Born from a singularity.

22

The stilly sounds of silences,
A bowl of polished earthenware,
The singing lark in the clear air,
A snowdrop bowed in plaintive prayer,
The cat meauwing on the stair,
The floral honeycombs of bumble bees,
Sharks prowling down the deepest seas,
The whoosh of water on the beach,
Sunrise streaming through the trees,
All born in the singularity.

23

Thirteen point seven billion years ago,
Is such a long, long way to go
And time is slow, is slow, is slow
But in the radiance of Consciousness
Nothing, nothing is left to chance,
For all things aspire to persevere
In their own being, in their own dance,
The Nonpareil, par excellence,
Made our Planet Earth, the masterpiece,
The jewel in the singularity.

24

Yes. All-There-Is is One and Whole,
An eternal, continuously-creating Soul
Interconnecting instantaneously,
Interwoven everywhere day and night,
Flowing in paradigms of shadow and light,
All things burning in the flames of desire,
All interacting in all other's dependence
In Creation's superabundant exuberance,
All from an Absolute Consciousness,
All from a singularity.

25

We must allow for the miraculous
Even when the testimony may be
Beyond all scientific probability
Because all Creation is real, wonder-filled,
And the suspension of disbelief
Must at times be the better choice,
Because its magic shimmers before our eyes,
And sweet harmonies resonate in its voice.
Now Mister Reader, you know what you know.
So what was that singularity?

Chapter Two

The Grand Unified Epoch, The Universe in its Infancy.

*"There is no smallest among the small and no largest among the large
but always something smaller and something still larger."*
Anaxagoras
*"It is rather fantastic to realise that the laws of physics can
describe how
everything was created in a random quantum fluctuation out of
nothing."* Alan Guth

1

The Universe in its infancy,
From zero to ten to the minus thirty-five,
A fraction of the first second we call time,
Absolute uniformity rhymed.
A single quantum system where
In some shape or form or size,
In some disguise we were all there!

2

The Universe in its infancy,
Diffusing from that singularity,
Saw energy and matter's equivalence
At one with Absolute Consciousness.
The four forces that we know today,
Gravity, electromagnetic and the nuclear pair
Were all unified in a singular way.

3

The Universe in its infancy
Was a womb of infinite possibilities,
With limitless energy potentialities,
And unimaginable properties.
In pre-geometrical space time
An ovum set the sperm alive.
Fertilization. Creation was the child.

4

The Universe in its infancy
Had All-There-Is metamorphosed
In ten millionths of a trillionth
Of a trillionth of a trillionth of a second,
At a thousand trillion, trillion
Degrees of candescence,
Into a Universe with a wavelength a millionth
Of a billion, billion, billionth of a centimetre!

5

The Universe in its infancy
Was driven by explosive energy

And forces indistinguishable
With an exotic mix of particles, anti-particles,
Creating and annihilating,
Expanded exponentially,
At speeds that are unimaginable,
With slight variations in density.

6

The Universe in its infancy
Began expanding from a billion times
Smaller than our dear little proton
To something like a marble,
From a wrinkled sphere to a smoothie.
As to where Dark Matter and Energy
Lurked at that time is anyone's guess
But they had to be there too in the mess.

7

The Universe in its infancy
Saw all four forces separate.
Gravity would go on its own way.
The strong nuclear force was frozen out.
This would trigger out inflation,
And the electroweak force would liberate
The weak, radioactive nuclear force
And the electromagnetic one.

8

The Universe in its infancy
Had fundamental uniformity.
The Cosmological Constants are so,

So finely tuned, their probability so, so low,
Each making the universe so hard to know
Yet they made our existence possible,
One in which our lives could thrive.
Constants that allow us be alive and survive,
Their values conducive to our lives.

9

The universe in its infancy,
Microcosmic to macrocosmic
Hides an unimaginable mystery;
That's the early uniformity
That led to the nonpareil Planet Earth,
And beyond, the voluptuous Universe,
Emanating and designed
From a Supreme Consciousness,
Inflating faster than the speed of light.

10

The Universe in its infancy
Was born out of that Consciousness,
A transcendent ocean of mystical light,
With bubbles that would be
Faraway galaxies eventually,
All interlaced and raddled in wreaths,
One of the bubbles our own.
Our island galaxy was on the go
In this cosmic archipelago.

11

The Universe in its infancy

Saw space separate too quickly
To arrive at thermal equality,
So a slowdown earlier on made sure
All came to a similar temperature.
Then a brief burst of rapid inflation,
Repulsive gravity, in that brief span,
Allowed uniform, spacial expansion.
The grand adventure had begun.

Chapter Three

The Locals in our Neighbourhood

UNIT ONE THE MILKY WAY

> *"Continuous as the stars that shine,*
> *And twinkle on the Milky Way…"*
> William Wordsworth

> *"We had the sky, up there, all speckled with stars, and we used to lay*
> *on our backs and look up at them, and discuss about whether they was*
> *made, or only just happened."*
> Mark Twain

1

Our own galaxy, the Milky Way,
Studded with palaces where the gods stay,
Like a disc-shaped grinding wheel in a mill
We follow its spiralling twirling still.

2

This is the galaxy where we are.
Built of four hundred billion stars

One hundred thousand light-years long,
Where our little Solar System belongs.

3

With oodles and oodles of nebulae
In its massive, sparkling Catherine wheel,
Twirling billions, billions of stars,
Dancing cosmological reels.

4

Pirouetting fantails unravelling out
To the circumference, whirling about,
Where most of these stars should be slung away.
But no! They seem to stay, to stay.

5

Held in Dark Matter's grasp? Even so?
Six times stronger than visible matter.
Outermost stars speed on too fast!
Whatever! Maybe! We just don't know.

6

Its pinwheel ponderously turns
As its bejewelled spirals burn,
With young blue stars in its nursery
Cawled in placental nebulosity.

7

A Black Hole, of mass three billion Suns,
Has swept the inner region clean
Whose gravity wheels all in scorching rotation
In a bulge of red and yellow starscene.

8

In its outer rims luminous stars are packed.
A secret lurks in its darkest heart.
Double trouble, a figure of eight,
The Fermi Bubbles fiercely gyrate,

9

Gamma rays from the galactic plane,
The highest energy photons we know,
But crisscrossing at our galaxy's core,
Blown from this super massive Black Hole,

10

Like the power of thousands of supernovae,
Centred it seems on nothingness.
Astrophysicists unanimously confide
"We don't know nothing. It's anyone's guess."

11

In one of those fantails where we lay our scene
Lies the Solar System, settled, serene,
And that yellow star we call the Sun
In a whirlpool of violences was born.

UNIT TWO THE SUN

"In Greek myth, Icarus flew too high and his wings melted. What is the moral?
Don't fly too close to the Sun? Or is it, as I choose to believe: build better wings."
Stanley Kubrick

1

The darling Sun, at break of day,
Sweeps across gardens with golden rays,
From prominences, flames of fire,
That swirl from the broiling photosphere
And some of its particles flung our way
Are charged curtains that ricochet

Off our paint-splattered palate atmosphere
And glow into shimmering aurorae.

2

At sunrise, glimmering stars go sleep,
Sunset's red sky disappears.
Until curtains of twinkling skies appear,
Glowing and lovely and dark and deep.
In swirling mists, moon witches rise,
The ghosts of the dreaded dead arise,
Foxes' chill incantations, cries,
As asteroids shoot across moonlit skies.

3

A four-billion-year-old main-sequence star,
Our Sun was stamped and hammered.
A plasmic adolescent in a nebula
Accreting matter with a violent temper.
A mottled ball of luminous plasma,
Billions of tons of mostly hydrogen,
Made from the slow collapse of clouds
That melted, condensed in a molten round.

4

The Sun set alight by nuclear fusion
Of hydrogen atoms burnt to helium,
Pouring electromagnetic radiation
From the core of nuclear reactions.
A tortured core, fifteen million degrees,
The Sun has burned two per cent of its whole,
Yet such is the density of this small patch
That it holds about half its gigantic mass.

5

Particles jumping, colliding and bumping,

Bouncing off in random directions,
Zigzagging, straggling, meandering about,
Over and back and down and out.
Nucleosynthesis converting
Matter to energy in fractions of seconds,
In a proton—proton chain reaction,
Again and again and again and again.

6

It takes about ten million years
For photons to reach the exosphere
And sail away when once set free
On a startling voyage through infinity.
When the Sun shrinks, the pressure increases,
More fusion, more energy releases,
The Sun swells from the heat increase,
Then cools. Self-regulating expediencies.

7

A radiation zone at two million degrees
Releases from outer photospheres
Cataclysmic, violent heat,
Mottled and pinking orange peel.
The chromosphere sends fireballs out,
Millions miles from the solar corona,
Like a gigantic convection zone,
With sudden spinacles broiling about.

8

Stretching out from corona bubbles,
Looping quakes, seismic ripples,
Orange-red flares, super faculae,
Prominences and sheets of stipples.
Massive ejections to outer space,

Geomagnetic storms of gamma rays,
Solar winds, zillions of particles,
All creating the Sun's irradiance,
9
Topping a million kilometres an hour,
Embracing our planet the way a bird
Gathers its wings around its eggs,
While our magnetosphere, our atmosphere,
Deflects danger harmlessly away,
Streaming clouds of protons, electrons,
Digitalising beautiful aurorae,
The scrawled signature of a Deity.
10
Aurora Borealis, Aurora Australis,
Spirits in Arctic, Antarctic skies.
Spectral neutrinos fly straight through us,
Zillions, zillions, all the livelong day.
Night time and zillions rise up through us
Where in our beds asleep we lay
From under the floorboards,
Untouchable rays.
11
These elemental energies from our darling Sun
Break free to wander near or far
Ready to make a new planet, new star,
Or be part of my private integrity
For the elements that make up you and me
Were made in a star's laboratory.
Ten thousand trillion cells. That's Me!
All working together in harmony.

Remember our darling Sun is the womb,
The genesis and gentle nursery
Of all that Existence-Has-Come-To-Be
And all our labour strives to understand
That mystery, it's Longing-To-Be,
A precinct beyond the particle,
The fields of force, the geometry
Of space-time, matter, energy and gravity.

13

Sunlight is the secret of our existence.
It unravelled Life and Being and Us,
As it radiated from this creative ball
At three hundred thousand k a second,
A kind of speed limit for us all!
The only word for it, absurd!
In the time it takes to say a word,
Think of the distance this light would traverse.
In the time it takes to say a verse,

14

Or in an hour, a day, a week,
A month, a year, - no one could speak
Such distances where light beams bend
Into where all recitation ends,
Beyond the beyonds,
Where conjecture ends.
It's the Light of our life, all life that we see,
A blue-green photonic mystery!

15

The molten Sun at six thousand degrees
With a shimmering corona one million degrees!

That's as hot as hot can be!
How on earth can this possibly be?
Just another part of the mystery.

ENVOI----THE SUN'S ENDING

"A time to be born and a time to die."
Ecclesiastes 3:1

All stars live with uncertainties,
Written in stone, their own Doomsdays,
Like our own darling, luminous Sun
Which will have its date with destiny.

One day it surely will fade away,
As a white dwarf with coloured environs
In a beautiful planetary nebula,
Like raindrops, its scattered cosmic rays.

Someday five billion years in time,
Someday when helium burning ceases
It will cool to a solid carbon sphere,
A glinting, diamond masterpiece

Crystallised to a White Dwarf lease,
Surrounded by an expanding gas release.
Hard to imagine all human relations
Is one of the cosmological equations

Loosed in the maelstrom of Creation,
Yet out of this incredible possibility
Grew the tremendous human reality
And the origins of life's incredible story.

Here we are in all our glory.
Alleluia, alleluia, alleluia.

UNIT THREE THE SOLAR SYSTEM

*"In the Solar System all the planets are in the same plane. They're all
going around
in the same direction. It's perfect, you know. It's gorgeous. It's almost
uncanny."*
Geoffrey Marcy

Five billion years ago, in a ghostly nebula,
From energetic material immensities
Flung from the remnants of a collapsed star,
In matter clouds, the Solar System came to be.

A slow spinning protoplanetary disc
Of particles clumping, larger, larger,
From the billions of rocky chunks flung out
Into the emptiness about.

Chunks grow to boulders,
Misshapen spheres,
Some curl back and orbit around
The protosun, scattering outbound.

Weathered by icy, rocky asteroids,
Faster contracting, faster colliding,
Cosmic crunching, merging debris,
Creating planetessimals.

Capturing gasses, clinging rocks,
For tens of millions of millions of years,
Grabbing, condensing, clumping together,
Crashing spectacular violences.

Collisions, asteroids, hotter, hotter,
More accretion of metals, rocks,
To rocky giants, circling a protosun,
Larger, larger, slash and burn.

Merging, fragmenting and unceasing,
Ever violent, ever increasing,
All in material quantitativeasing,
Hydrogen, dust and gasses baking.

Gravity grabbing the finitessimals
And electromagnetic particles.
All in an anticlockwise rotation
Creating order from the mayhem.

Heat burning off the light gas floor,
As all cools to a liquid molten core.
Most gasses lost to interstellar space,
Only a fraction of it all remains.

Some rubble escaped into whirling rings
Colder, colder, an asteroid belt.
The ice-rich material all around
Began to coalesce into satellites.

Chapter Four

Earth, Third Planet from the Sun

"Blue and beautiful", the spacemen say, *"Our planet is, from far away."*

Through the clouds, sunlight comes shining through.
But look! The rest of the sky is blue.
The atmosphere scatters its rays of light
Like a gardener scattering seeds,
Or an ocean scattering water beads
And the blue wavelengths are in between
The wavelengths for indigo and for green.
See cerulean azure seeping through
And that is why the sky is blue.

Clouds scatter the sunlight too,
The shimmering droplets diffract, diffuse,
Sunlight shafting from drop to drop,

More, more dense, and more intense,
As millions of little drops condense,
More diffusion, light goes white,
And that is why the clouds are white.
When the light leaves the clouds of rain
It keeps a memory of where it's been.

That's the little matter called Consciousness.
Reflections shine on the teeming seas,
Luxurient meadows and fertile trees.
Earthrise, over a lunar horizon, the moon's
Moon dancing to a watery tune.
Circling, tilted, for summer's glow,
Away, for winter's falling snow.
Earth, the oddball, in planetary light,
In summer's heat, in moonlit night.

In Mother Nature's cornucopia of old,
The darling element, the gold,
Stardust, from the solar furnace,
Rivetting order out of chaos.
Joining the dots of all aspects of life.
And the seed essentials of Life were laid,
In Mother Earth when she was made.
Out of the rubble of exploding suns,
This wonder grew, the Special One.

Heavy rocks sunk to the molten core
And mixing, created a jewellery store
Of gems and stones and magical ore.
Diamond, emerald, sapphire, pearl,

Ruby, agate, amethyst, beryl,
Garnet, topaz, onyx, and coral,
Spangled rosette and chatelaine opal,
Illumined finesse and flamboyant rouge,
Symmetrical peacock and arabesque plume.

Oxygen, light, and evolution,
Beauty, love and revolution.
The oceanic crust is rather thin,
Continental crust has thicker skin.
This is fragmented into plates
That collide and buckle-up himalayes.
The oceans cool and lubricate
The movable techtonic plates.

An Earth with variety, diversity,
Complexity, and above all, humanity.
An Earth where astonishing differences
Became the terrestrial commonplace.
Earth and the Moon had the same birth,
Same isotopic materials as Earth.
Cataclysmic impacts, cosmic debris,
Swept up over millions and millions of years.
Swept up from rubble and litter collisions,
Bombardment, cataclysmic origins.

How it could store the H2O
Four billion years, we'll never know.
But store it did and creating me
Became a possibility.
A nest for the improbable, the guest

Appearance of existences.
Incontrovertible physics, astronomy,
With all the antropic principles we know
Show that the Universe was made for me.

But know it was a long, long time ago,
Before the spectre, sapiens homo,
Rose to his feet, rose from the shallows,
Strange beginnings slowly followed,
Rising to wisdom, philosophy,
The genes of all the humanities,
The genes of magnanimity,
Of thought, of justice, of music, of poetry,
Chemistry, science, astronomy,
Metaphysics and biology.

With fire and air and water and soil,
Earth is the planetary nonpareil.
Beauty, O, beauty, is everywhere
In water, in soil, in fire, in air.
Creative imaginations are inspired
By air, by water, by soil, by fire.
The marvellous darknesses that matter
Secrete in fire, air, soil and water.
Every patch is a mirroring foil
For the beauty in water, air, fire and soil.

Planet Earth,
The beautiful nonpareil.

Chapter Five

What is the Origin of Existence?

UNIT ONE A COSMIC DIRECTOR.

*"To lift up the hands in prayer gives glory to God, but the man with
a dungfork in his hand, a woman with a slop-pail, gives him
glory too."*
GM Hopkins

The Universe had few secrets now!
These radio-wave filaments of light
Reveal the secrets of ancient times,
Give us glimpses like screens of flickering snow
That floated down since billions of years ago.

Four hundred million microwave photons
Floating through each cubic metre of space,
Like a film made by a Cosmic Director
When the cosmos was but a juvenile actor.
A Universe smooth as a baby's face!

What Director of Photography
Could mix the filters to usher in
Such cosmological uniformity?
Where independent cosmic domains
Spoke the same language, sang the same refrains,

All on infinitely stretched out plains,
Sharing a common temperature,
While receding galaxies in flight
With no limits as to how space swells
Drift away faster than the speed of light?

What Cosmic Mother, Consciously,
Mapped birth, infancy, childhood years,
The crawl through aons to maturity,
Expanding isotropically,
To today's high degrees of symmetry?

A revolutionary cartography
Of past, present, future history,
Along the calendar since Time was released
To its end when Time will cease,
Found in reverberations from the Big Bang.

UNIT TWO OUR EXISTENCE

*"I have seen the moment of my greatness flicker, And I have seen
the eternal Footman hold my coat and snicker, And, in short, I was
afraid."*
TS Eliot

Come back! Let's drink the native brew,
All cosmology is a local view.
A cosmos congenial to all the needs
For our actual existence here.

Why should we all exist in it?
Why all existence for our benefit?
The universe exists for human life,
A precondition for all space and time.

That would seem to imply to me
A universe made for you, for me.
Intelligent life could not exist
Unless a Progenitor decided it.

Nought left to chance, no dice to roll,
A Designer of definite, genetic laws,
And a biophilic cosmology.
Who could have tuned it all so fine?

Could there be an Omniscient Divine?
So who needs faith when we have physics
That undeniably proves the faith?
Who needs physics when we have faith?

This Tremendous Lover, trusting, innate,
Its absolute vision, Its certainty
Of All-That-Would-Not
And All-That-Would-Be,

That we slowly unfold through astronomy,
Chemistry, physics and biology,
With all strings gloriously tuned
To create Perfection's overture.

So here we are, and we clearly see
The universe as it is meant to be.
A Universe greater than we can see
Beyond our limits towards eternity,

Buzzing with possibilities,
Like bubbles in spacetime's limitless seas.
This complex world we know, don't know,
Must be required for Earth to be so.

The Planet Earth, ideal for life,
The single home where we can survive.
That we are alive is no great surprise!
Our presence the one essential. Look! See!

If it were different, we wouldn't be.
Our real existence, its feasibility,
Was the one precondition that must be.
Without observers, Creation would not be.

UNIT THREE THE MYSTERY

> *"I cannot forecast to you the action of Russia. It is a riddle*
> *wrapped in a mystery inside an enigma."*
> Winston Churchill
> *"He who bends to himself a joy*
> *Does the winged life destroy;*

But he who kisses the joy as it flies
Lives in eternity's sunrise."
William Blake

And as all matter stretches out in space,
The emptiness will become a cold, cold place.
Time past, time present, both combined,
Tell us how future is determined.

Space past, space present both instruct
The kind of future space will construct.
Now is the still point in between
All-That-Will-Be and All-That-Has-Been.

Consciousness always is aware
Of All-That-There-Will-be
Whatever the conditions
Of What-Life-Seems-To-Be.

All things that exist imprint
Their singular significance
In the cosmic parish where
They keep a living presence,

And they extend creative
Possibilities, essences,
With the definitive reality
Of their personal presences

So, in their own individual,
Immeasurable way
They enhance the bank of reality
Which all Consciousness animates

34

As the universe moves inexorably
Towards its own coherence,
To higher states of subtlety
Along the Spectrum of Consciousness.

Let's not forget another mystery.
Four per cent matter is all we see,
Dark Matter is about twenty-three,
Dark Energy something like seventy-three.

So where does that leave you and me?
Yes, scratching in incredulity
At the loose end of a galaxy.
That's all we see of eternity.

We are the children of nebulae,
Born out of magma and stellar explosions,
Primordial hydrogen, helium,
In thermonuclear fusions.

We are stardust made into flesh.
Elements like helium, oxygen, carbon
Were forged inside the stars that were born
And died long before Planet Earth.

All the elements from that violent strife
Are the keys to the secret of our lives.
If this is all we think we know,
What Cosmic Creator made it so?

We wonder why we wonder why
We wonder why we wonder…

Why this cosmological So-And-So
Created the merciless tearing asunder
Of atoms, of matter and quarks
And lightning and thunder,

Ripping out particles, over and under,
Pummelling galaxies with order and blunder,
And ripping itself with exquisite plunder.
A Universe laced with pernicious wonder

That still could play tender serenades,
And sculpt such magical everglades,
Write poems of beauty, sorrow and joy,
And paint such an enigmatic sky?

We wonder why we wonder why
We wonder why we wonder...
Who knows what future lies before or
Behind the supernatural door?

What sweet surprise may be our fate?
Or something none could anticipate?
Another kind of time and space
That helps us hope, helps us keep faith?

Another kind of space and time?
Where peace and consolation rhyme
And where Love, the transcendent Consummate,
Is the singular, illimitable Sublime?

Chapter Six

Planet Earth in One Day

"As we look out into the Universe and identify the many accidents of physics
and astronomy that have worked together to our benefit, it almost seems
as if the Universe must in some sense have known we were coming."
Freeman Dyson
"Science has as yet thrown no light on the far higher problem of the
essence or origin of life." Charles Darwin
"Life is good and bad. Mostly and."
Diogenes

1

Life on Earth distilled to one day.
Midnight was four point seven billion years ago.
The Earth is a red-black smouldering ball
Of molten rock, a dull red glow,
With galactic debris in a noxious stew,
Exhaling carbon dioxides,
Swirling, clumping matter and gas,
Pelted by comets and meteorites.

2

Gravity holds the atmosphere.
Through surface crusts volcanoes thrust,
Ultra-violet rays floundering down,
Lightning zinging through the cloud bursts.
This lightning and ultraviolet light
Break up hydrogen molecules,
That recombine instantaneously,
Dissolving in oceans of organic soup.

3

And early that day a massive asteroid
Out of the blue smashed the young Earth
With an angular, thundering belt
Ripping its heart with liquifying impact.
Heavy bits fused, light ones ejected
Out in a disc orbiting round
Then cooled, cooled and solidified
As the debris congealed into the Moon

4

And left Earth, one supercontinent,
With a tilt in its axis of rotation
Of twenty-three point five degrees.
Sun, Earth and Moon locked in orbital dance.
Did this wonder of wonders happen by chance?
Or was it the gift uncertain seasons bring
In winter, autumn, summer and spring?

5

Time's flow is slow, is slow, is slow.
A million years is a long way to go
But four point seven billion or so?
Each hour is millions, the hours go by.

Harping minutes out of number fly.
Rifts, continental drifts, split and scatter,
Techtonics wrench and meteors cluster
Into volcanoes and mountains of matter.

6

Stirrings of life, the smallest units,
With the impetus to create the Conscious,
An Awareness that permeates all that is,
Through the interaction of atomic tricks,
The planet fundamentally alive!
Each atomic unit containing inherently
The knowledge of all entities
With the Wave Function guiding the particle.

7

Call this the Quantum Potential.
This is the world of the very small.
All atoms with the same dictionary,
All knowing the same code
From generation to generation
While a fragment of genetic information
Is sometimes adopted by a random cell
Which will call it its very own.

8

This subatomic Consciousness raised itself
Up to the biological shelf
And a wider Awakening had begun
With the single-celled bacteria
That became aware of a belvedere,
Inclusive, grander and more clear,
Integrating Mindfulness
In that ever-deepening Consciousness.

9

The Earth is a molecular Garden of Eden,
As it cools, cools for a billion years.
At five in the morning, radiation
Seeps in volcanoes and water-green seas,
Creating greenhouse gasses here.
Those stirrings of life were humble then,
Inorganic fragments recombining
In slowly increasing complexities.

10

Cooling, the Earth solidified
While continental lands appeared.
It is an oxygen-free arena,
A nursery for single-celled bacteria.
Until one, fine, sunny morning,
On an inexplicable Designer day,
A molecule woke up, made a copy of itself,
The crude ancestor of DNA.

11

Whether from germs in meteorites,
In bacteria, microbes and algae,
Life crawled where it could survive and thrive,
Replicating at a furious rate.
From then to three in the afternoon,
About two billion years in time,
Mutations evolved varieties
Such as those in fossil stromatolites.

12

Up to ten that morning, two billion years,
Trillions, quadrillions swimming together,
Life happened and it happened once,

In the same gene pool, hell for leather.
Evolution was slow, was slow, was slow,
For the bacteria-like blue-green algae,
And life just wanted it to be so, be so.
Fossil formations tell us so.

13

From a living, incredible, genetic trick,
Where a little cluster of chemicals which
Were given a subtle primordial whisk
By a Designer's delicate switch,
All living things originated there.
Bacterial rocks fill the shallows,
Bloomed, blossomed, sang and danced,
The blue-green algae drank, drank

14

Abundances of nitrogen,
Spitting out globules of oxygen.
The atmosphere an acidic stew,
Criss-crossed with stunning lightning strikes
Zinging through whorling noxious fumes.
In other words, it stank, it stank.
After ten o'clock, better classes of cells,
Multicellular eukaryotes,

15

The wonders of sophistication,
With shoulder sacks of DNA, all day, all day,
A nucleus with tiny organelles,
As hungry mithochondria
Kept spitting out oxygen that sank, sank,
And rusted down the primordial seas,
Which in turn, oxidised ocean-rust,
While methane moulded an ozone-must.

16

Hoovering carbon dioxide, water and light,
They invented photosynthesis.
Their ghosts sleep in those stromatolites.
The gigantic supercontinent yanked, yanked,
The techtonic plates as it cooled, cooled,
Oceans filling the empty pools.
Oxygen growing, filling the atmosphere,
Million on million it cools, cools,

17

While ozone filtered ultraviolet rays.
The oxide-rusted waters turned blue.
Slow learners, yet they learned well, so well,
How to make entities visible.
They gobbled up the iron and manganese
Locked inside rocks, with consummate ease,
Down at the bottom of the blue-green seas
And threw up carbohydrates.

18

About the time for the nine o'clock news
Six hundred million years ago,
Miscellaneous promiscuous cells, cells,
Discerning new biological phenomena,
Raised their levels of Consciousness
To discover the secret of sentient lives
And so began their slow reveal. Reveal.

19

The planet begins to teem with life
In the suddenly, flourishing, Cambrian time.
Simple animal forms were supplanted
By the clawed, feathered, scaled and armoured,

Blueprints of the wonderful creatures
We see all around us today, today,
Which are tinkerings to ancient designs,
Modern versions of antique paradigms.

20

Sea-bed scavengers came alive.
Nine thirty, The Late Late. It's the trilobites live!
Exquisite adaptations came in sight, in sight!
Species appeared, then flickered out
And insects made pioneering flights.
This the springtime of life's history,
With little creatures to beat the band,
About ten in the evening of our day.

21

Millions in herds trawl the sea sand
With heads and tails and limbs galore and
Exquisite adaptations came and
Five past ten and the worms are crawling and
Millipedes were sprinting past and
Lichens are clinging to the rocks and
Jellyfish blobs are bobbing in seas and
Winged insects sail the evening breeze.

22

Make way for sea plants and for fauna,
For those up to now restricted in seas
Learned to crawl and to colonise land,
Invertebrates, amphibians in water, on land.
Ten o'clock. Forty-five million years ago
Fish with jaws began to thrive,
While immobile filtering feeders vanish.
Goodness gracious, snakes alive!

23

Aquatic curlicues are slithering by.
Darting fishes learn how to survive
These writhing, spiralling reptiles.
Some clamber up rocks to colonise,
And live on plants as continents slide,
Techtonics crush as mountains rise
And the massive forces of nature connive
To ensure the hapless are buried alive!

24

And many another species died.
Oh! Listen to their querulous cries!
While waters filled the hollowed gaps
Like oceans that you see on map, on maps.
Eleven o'clock. The dinosaurs thrive.
That great intellectual long since dead!
Brains in his cranium, brains in his spine!
He could think in his arse, think in his head!

25

He could think twice before he dined!
His argumentation was precise!
Weighing up a-priori intent
Against a-posteriori content!
He argued from different premises!
Allosaurus, diplodocas,
And the braindead Apatosaurus,
Monstrous, imbecile, chimera hordes.

26

But will the dinosaurs survive?
Creatures crawl with legs and toes.
Carboniferous forests rise

And reach out to oxygenated blue skies.
Oceans and ice-sheets come and go.
Look! See the winged dragonflies dive
Up and out from their anchorage
And beautifully take to sudden flight.

27

Meteorites crush the day into night
Blotting out sunlight for years or so
And there were mass extinctions too,
In the Permian Age the worst of these.
Eleven forty. Trilobites, dinosaurs obliterated
With most species on land, in skies and seas.
Those mongrel brutes with cerebral limits
Survive for only forty minutes!

28

The scarred and limping survivors
Took millions, millions of years to recover.
Twenty minutes are left in our day.
The age of mammals was on the way.
But all the while, the while, the while,
After billions of years of evolution,
Aeons of catastrophic revolution,
From molecules born in stellar events,

29

Through atmospheric pulses and vents,
Through species born and species extinct,
Two hundred million years to the day,
A shrew with teeth like grains of sand,
Rows of incisors, canines and molars,
A skull with cells and ears and eyes,
Mammals' limbs and shoulders and glands
Set out on its long and royal progress

30

To reign supreme in the promised isle.
This was the day we all highfived.
Man, in our beautiful paradise.
Ten million years ago,
The planet cools with flowering grasses,
All sorts of mammals and birds are alive
Followed by primates and hominoids
Locomoting in a lumbering way.

31

In savannahs, some gracile, slender creatures,
Some sturdy, muscular and robust,
Wore funny noses and chimp-like features.
Up in the trees orangutans,
Ancestral gorillas, chimpanzees, apes.
Three million years ago or more,
Lucy, one of the first ancestors known,
Came down from the trees, settled,

32

With a brain and hands to fling a stone.
With guile, with cunning and swift feet,
Parental hominins became
The two-legged masters of the forest floor
And after homo this and homo that,
Homo erectus left Africa
One point five million years ago,
Slowly found Europe and Asia,
Went wherever the winds would blow,

33

Found cunning strategies for survival,
Hunted, made fire, made tools,

And of all the humanoid varieties
Homo sapiens alone survived.
We know because in its DNA
We read the blueprint of his life,
For cells retain the vital clues
Back to the beginning of its time.

34

Sapiens learned to cherish community,
The young, the old, the infirm and the frail.
Growing in forests, sleeping near trees,
Oh! How lovely are trees' rich affinities!
Leaves harvest sunlight, water in roots,
Sheltering all with a languid grace.
They stole the carbohydrates
And recycled them in their place.

35

In a nettle a carbon dioxide molecule
Combines with water to make a sugar.
The stolid donkey gobbles the nettle,
Digests the sugar molecule.
This releases enough energy
So the donkey can whisk his tail.
Then he converts the sugar
Into carbon dioxide and happily exhales.

36

And every flower has an electric field,
Sensory abilities to lure the bees
And every root communicates underground
Responding to elemental touch and sound,
And his master's voice will never fail
To elicit harrumph, a bark or a wag of its tail!

Such aspects of Consciousness
Show environmental Awarenesses.

37

Plants and humans live in communion
Inhaling each other's exhalations,
A cosmic balance where each is giving
Mouth-to-mouth resuscitation.
Still, humans, it seems, were poor zookeepers.
The dodo, black mamo, hopping mouse,
Bachman warbler, flightless wren
And the Carolina parakeet witnessed this!

38

After twenty-three hours, fifty-eight minutes,
Forty-three seconds, as day expired
Homo Sapiens found his feet...
Travelling north, south, west and east.
A hundred thousand years ago,
Original, thinking, with intuitive skill,
Made an axe, the newest technology,
To pound, to smash, to split and to kill.

39

One minute and seventeen seconds
Is the compass of all human history.
And the twinkling of recorded time
Is of an evanescent brevity.
And so we come to the end of day
And time past is contained in time present
And time future stretches far away...
O! So little time to wonder why.

40

We wonder why, we wonder why,
We wonder why we wonder...

Chapter Seven

From Conscious Particles to our World

UNIT ONE FOSSILS AND FIELDS AND CONSCIOUSNESS

"The whole drift of my education goes to persuade me that the world of our present consciousness is only one out of many worlds of consciousness that exist."
William James

Each fossil is a fragment of the history
Of our lovely planet as she goes
And our planet is but a fragment
Of the wonder-filled cosmos.

The fossils we find in bodies and rocks
Are planetary calendars and clocks.
DNA, our common ancestor,

Mutated, evolved and swapped some species
In a hierarchical architecture,
Small to larger entities, new defining properties,
Each one more complex than its parts.

Changes came inexorably,
Now measured in radiocarbon dating,
In rocks, in water and in life's features,
All changes Consciously interlinked
Between land and air and water creatures
For matter and mind share equivalence,
Inseparable, infused, Longing-To-Become.

Consciousness is the guiding school
For every atom, each molecule
Like the artist that paints the canvas white
Then enriches with stirring breezes in trees,
Startling, blowsy leaves, heaving seas,
Till the masterpiece unfolds in the light
Of his aesthetic Consciousness.

Oh! Nature is stranger and more fraught,
Than all your physicists ever thought!
All particles have a pulsating nature,
All matter is pulsating fields,
Trillions of notes on the overture,
Invisible, intangible harmonies
In the opera of probabilities.

All Consciousness is pulsating too,
All matter is energy Resonance,

And it gives our seeming three dimensions
The appearance of permanence.
Creatures with cells and genes,
Colonies all aware of each other
And functioning all together.

Organs and tissues together in harmony
To ensure individual integrity
That communicate and interact,
Interconnecting impenetrably,
As they continually divide and die
In a strangely intricate harmony
Of that all-pervading Consciousness.

UNIT TWO THE ATOM, THE KING OF INFINITE SPACE.

"I could be bounded in a nutshell
And count myself the king
of infinite space
Only I have bad dreams."
William Shakespeare
If you were to reduce scientific history to one important
statement it would be: "All things are of atoms made."
Richard Feynman

Mothers are always right, they say.
My mother would say with gentle grace,
"Son, you're only a wasted space."
If only she knew how right she was!

If you squeeze out all the empty space
Of all the atoms in the human race
Then humanity would fill a claret vase,
Compressed like a neutron or quark-star place.

Quantum is dazzling in its precision.
Its physics found beauty in perfection
And mapped the infinitesimal seas,
On an incredible voyage of discoveries.

We get a humbling vision of our place
In the quantum nutshell, a tiny place.
Each atom has enough shells to enable
Its place on the Periodic Table.

A drop of water will tell you little
Of the goings-on deep down the sea,
But an atom reveals the secret life
Of all that exists fundamentally.

Atoms are completely impossible
From the point of view of classical,
But when you, o you, with them interact,
You end their dual "wave-particle" act

Because the wave function will collapse.
You end their schizophrenic pact!
They decide they will be sensible!
The atom's electrons are all identical.

Elements from one to ninety-two,
Has electrons wheeling, wheeling,

Whirling in seven concentric shells
Around the infinitesimal space.

Near the speed of light, they spin and chase
But electrons are never here or there,
More a cloud of being everywhere,
Never crossing intervening space!

Shell one, holds two, hydrogen, helium,
Shell two, eight, lithium to neon,
Shell three, eight, sodium to argon,
Shell four, eighteen, potassium to krypton,

Shell five, eighteen, rubidium to xenon,
Shell six, thirty-two, caesium to radon,
Shell seven, six, francium to uranium.
The same number of protons and neutrons.

Yes, yes, you might expect some confusion,
But no, all behave in sublime collusion.
Atoms are pretty indestructible
And follow beautiful quantum rules.

They join together as molecules
To create all visibles that exist,
Trillions, trillions in a leaf, in heather,
In a strand of hair, in a robin's feather,

In an eyelash, a moon, a splash in the sea,
In the indifferent corners of a galaxy,
In jasmine scents on the evening breeze,
In magnolia and eucalyptus trees,

In sunset isles washed in lakes of fire,
In the winged, buzzing, orchestral skies,
In the perilously teeming seas,
In quiescent beauty, in desire,

In the light of these words your eyes entertain—
Interpretations from your electrical brain—
In colonies of leaves, of minutiae,
That capture the light of the Sun, faraway,

That nuclear furnace that burns, burns,
To fuse molecular chains of elements,
Hydrogen into helium ones
All made from, yours truly, atoms.

Their structure yours, your darling Mom,
Cousin Josephine and Uncle Tom,
The stability of all things arises from
The enigmatic, invisible atom.

The atomic arcade is an empty place.
The central nucleus, one billionth of its space,
Confines the protons and neutrons
In each of which three quarks are intact.

Outside, infinitesimal electrons chase
And roam the endlessly empty place.
The atom is electrically neutral,
Electrons, protons keep equilibrium.

Protons and neutrons interplay,
Swapping charges, identities,
Interchanging their own roles
In the tiniest of tangencies,

A fraction millionth of a millionth.
O The microscopic drama dances
To the music of the quantum forces.
And all the atoms ever made

Billions of years old, are good as new.
Age does not degrade them,
They do not grow old as we grow old,
Yet our atoms are billions of years old.

The same as those in supernovae,
Collapsing, incandescent infernos,
Millions, millions of years ago,
Millions, millions of lightyears away.

All things are of atoms made.
All in the visible Universe.
Constructs of tiniest particles,
And the differences within depend

On the electrons, protons and neutrons.
The proton's positive electric charge
Is exactly equal, opposite the electron's.
A mystery no one understands.

Our dazzling electron can bilocate,
Be in a million sites at once,
Due to its magic wavelike face!
And the impenetrable penetrate!

And know another instantly
Quadrillions of light years away!
Unpredictable or doing sweet damn all
For diddlysquat reason all day!

Locked inside microscopic vaults
They shed their shackles, walk away,
Like alpha particles breaking out
In magic radioactive decay!

Radioactive dating tells us
Minute amounts of isotopes
Spontaneously decay
Into various other isotopes.

Quantum tunnelling, no doubt,
Here in this room, wherever that may be,
Eternillions humming in harmony.
But no visible quantum activity!

All "matter/energy" has Significance,
Fundamental Awarenesses
And all entities merge together
Mediated by a Consciousness.

All enfolding and unfolding in a continuous
Spectrum of levels of order,
Beautiful symmetry, seeming randomness,
Mediated by a Consciousness.

This instantaneous communication
Is an essential in a singular universe
Of Interpenetratedness, Wholeness,
Mediated by a Consciousness.

UNIT THREE WHAT EVERY PARTICLE KNOWS...

"Nothing is so simple it cannot be misunderstood."
Albert Einstein
"A tune beyond us as we are, yet nothing changed by the blue guitar;
Ourselves in the tune as if in space, yet nothing changed, except the place
Of things as they are and only the place as you play them, on the blue guitar..."
Wallace Stephens

Every electron knows
Where every other electron goes,
What every other electron is doing
In the Universe.

Every proton knows
Where every other proton goes,
What every other proton is doing
In the Universe.

Every neutron knows
Where every other neutron goes,
What every other neutron is doing
In the Universe.

Mind or Consciousness
Is inherent in all electrons
And it forces molecular complexes
To make particular choices.

Consciousness is the Being-There
And Becoming-More-Aware,
Knowing the possibilities
And knowing which to choose.

Between all fundamental particles
There exist vigilant Resonances,
Inseparable interconnectedness,
An elementary Consciousness,

All interpenetrating seamlessly,
Adjusting, readjusting endlessly,
Accommodating all inexplicably.

UNIT FOUR ATOMS AND THEIR POTENTIAL
ALIVE ALIVE OH!

"Love can tell, and love alone,
Whence the millions of stars were strewn,
And why each atom knows its own."
Robert Bridges

"Is the electron alive? Maybe it is! What sense would it make to say it is not? The electron must behave in all sorts of strange ways ... it cannot be understood but only be calculated. If you don't want to say it is alive say it is a total mystery."
David Bohm

To electrons whizzing around the nucleus
The proton must seem colossal,
The neutron a gigantic ball.
To us imperceptibly small.
One of the strangest mysteries of all.

Electrons should spiral in and down
In a mere hundred millionth of a second
But the protons hold the electrons in chains
With fierce electromagnetic attraction,
As they communicate, brain to brain,

Like a million sardines in a rounded shoal,
Each sardine knowing the right way to roll
Or thick-skinned elephants that synchronise,
Even when separated by miles
With inaudible fluttering between the eyes.

Electrons, subatomic, point-like fuzzballs,
At any one time in umpteen places,
Each wave corresponds to a particle,
Each particle behaving like a wave.
A mixed-up schizophrenic state.

So, an electron is a wave with a Wave Function,
States with a probability for existence.

The wave on digital wave rolls along
On an infinity of possible paths,
To arrive and be a point in one place!

Where it has been in between,
From a slit to a screen, is anyone's guess.
But it was, simultaneously,
Everywhere, along the wave,
Which filled the Universe instantaneously!

Weird? Yes, Weird. Believe you me!
The electron knows the path to choose,
It secretly explores every possible route!
These boyos know where they are going,
And they know when they're being watched!

They truly comprehend space and time,
Knowledge way beyond our knowing
Because they are Intelligent, Alive!
Akin with the primordial Consciousness
That sets all energies going.

Their wave/particle aspects contrive
To keep in touch with the Potential,
A deeper, sub-quantum level that thrives,
More subtle and more complex and
Down in the physicists' no-man's-land.

So, all existence is made of energies
And information that gives it shape.
Information there, is available everywhere

Through the Quantum Potential,
A sub-realm we only begin to appreciate.

The Quantum Wave Potential
Depends on every particle.
Hard to imagine yet to us accessible,
A realm where we, in living, see
Sprinklings of its multi-dimensional reality.

It is more complex than we can know it to be
Where all the potentialities
Are actual probabilities,
A domain interconnectedly Whole,
An aspect of the all-encompassing Soul.

Each of us part of this invisible,
Interpenetrating, intermeshed web.
What happens here, happens there
And instantaneously influences
At the deepest level what happens everywhere.

Spacetime and matter are elusive potentialities.
Consciousness creates our Reality
Out of the Wave Function Domain,
An incomprehensible reservoir,
An immeasurable underlay of light energy.

The Quantum Wave Potential
Is revealed to us through Consciousness,
The one and only sublimity,
The original, continuous miscellany
Of all energies and all existences.

UNIT FIVE IT'S WORTH REMEMBERING... ALL THINGS ARE OF ATOMS MADE

All things are of atoms made
In this simple, complex scenario,
Rolling the probability surges,
Misted with lines of electric pulses,
Like light from an infinitesimal sun.

O! How the electrons laughed and spun
Near the speed of light, they would prance and turn
In a quantum dance of perpetual fun,
While inside the nucleus' ambient view
The protons and neutrons clung like glue.

In each, trinomial quarks clung too
With a strong nuclear attractiveness,
A clinging greater than we can know,
The farther the stretch, the greater the draw,
Like your own private inverse square law.

In this infinitesimal scenario,
Mailed in triple bronze, heart to heart,
Clasped in embraces, never to part,
Quarks watch in awe the electrons' dance,
Whirling close to the speed of light,

Whizzing, whirring in and out
On the seemingly infinite roundabout
While the protons and electrons seem to be
Never oblivious, aware of one another,

No matter how far apart they may be.

An Awareness where particle antennae
Pick up Quantum Wave information,
So, each one knows the state of the whole,
Strangeness beyond our comprehension,
So, any event happening anywhere

Is instantaneously available everywhere.
It seems all matter is Alive
In subtleties no physics could contrive.
Take a deep breath. It does not fit.
It's not our country. But we live in it!

A Universe different to what we see
In spiders, butterflies, chimpanzees,
In finny and feathered creatures that abound,
On land, in flood, in skies, underground,
In apples, in kitchens, in blossoms, in trees,

In horrendous, gawky deformities,
In precious, sublime aesthetics,
In zoos, fish-ponds, menageries,
In communities of the republics
And in comical people like yous and mes.

UNIT SIX ALL THAT EXISTS ARE MADE OF FIELDS

(A field is usually called the Wave Function of the particle. This is a complex number and we have no way to sense it, unlike a real number that we can touch or smell or see.)

All that exists is made of fields.
Substances that spin through space,
Interconnecting everyplace.

All vibrations in collective fields
That we recognise as particles.
Fermions buzzing in quantum fields.

All interactive vacillations
In broken, rippling symmetries
That seem to know what living means.

Physicists know the numbers, the texts,
To read the superb hieroglyphics
Of modern-day particle physics.

The laws of physics have symmetries.
Look at the six-cornered snowflake.
Patterns repeated beautifully.

Rotate a circle. Where is the change?
Twirl a square. The square is still there!
Their changes we treat with indifference.

Still the forces of Nature arise from these

Because the simplest of symmetries
Can lead to most profound consequences.

Vibrations in boson fields, disguised, invisible to us,
Must be broken to acquire mass,
And stop them zipping off at light speed.

Low mass, high energy, wavelength compressed,
High mass, low energy, wavelength, immense.
Forces, mathematical, indifferent to the start.

A singing bird with a million volts zinging past
In the wire will louder sing for every plume
Indifferent to its circumstance.

Forces operate the same way
Whether you be a proton, say,
Asleep, dreaming on a mountain top

Or whizzing inside a cosmic ray
Through a galaxy many light years away.
The laws of physics have symmetries.

Interconnecting symmetries,
Resonances that cross-criss, criss-cross,
The underlying Consciousness.

All that exists are made of fields.

UNIT SEVEN PROBABILITIES.

Roll the dice. Add up the score.
Outcomes less likely, some outcomes more.
The Wave Function changes with passing time.
Momentum and position do not rhyme.

Uncertainty is their common feature.
The more you find one, the less the other.
These little buggers hop off anywhere,
And in the instant end up everywhere!

Uncertainty about position-velocity:
Miniscule for a plane at height,
Increasing for a bacterium,
But gigantic for an electron in flight.

Electrons can't share the same quantum state.
No two with the self-same energy.
Each one a tiny electric point.
You can't pin down an electron.

Chapter Eight

Complex Creatures make a Stand, Homo Sapiens Arrives

"The realization that one or a few genetic accidents made our human history possible will provide us with a whole new set of philosophical challenges to think about."
Svante Paabo
"The chess-board is the world, the pieces are the phenomena of the universe,
the rules of the game are the laws of Nature. The player on the other side is
hidden from us. We know his play is always fair, just and patient.
But we know, to our cost, that he never overlooks a mistake…"
Thomas Huxley

1
Planet Earth is the nurturing nest
For the improbable, the guest
Appearance of existences.
Incontrovertible physics and astronomy,

Show the Universe was made for you and me.
Complex creatures make a stand.

2

All sorts of life in abundance thrives
In every conceivable niche.
With fire and air and water and soil,
Earth is the planetary nonpareil
For complex creatures to make a stand.

3

Beauty, O, beauty, everywhere
In water, earth, fire and air.
Creative imaginations inspire
In air, water, earth and fire
Where complex creatures make a stand.

4

The marvellous darknesses that matter
In fire, air, earth and water,
Faith, hope and love find birth
In water, fire, air and earth,
As complex creatures make a stand.

5

Down the procreative roads
Where beautiful, intricate creatures grow,
Flora, fauna, herds and flocks,
And the teeming waters of Being flow,
Complex creatures make a stand.

6

It was a long, long time ago,
Before the spectre, sapiens homo,
Rose to his feet, rose from the shallows,
Strange beginnings slowly followed,
As complex creatures make a stand.

7

Homo grew from some chemical brew,
Eyelets skulking behind fronds
In warm and cosy little ponds,
And after millennia of evolution,
Complex creatures make a stand.

8

Magical human pregnancy, birth,
Create elaborate human parts,
Eye and ear and finger and heart,
Marvels beyond the biologies,
As complex creatures make a stand.

9

Homo sapiens had the sense
To make language, culture and poetry
And catch the scent of evolution,
Variation, survival and replication,
As complex creatures make a stand.

10

Rising to wisdom, philosophy,
The genes of all the humanities,
The genes of magnanimity,
Of thought, justice, science, sagacity.
Complex creatures make a stand.

11

Now we linger on the cosmic shores,
Wanderers, we open doors,
And walk out into the darkness
With an eye for enlightened radiances.
Complex creatures make a stand.

12

Into the realms of love, of ideals,
Marvels of a transcendent kind,
With the sublime wonder, the intelligent mind,
Bearing the hallmarks of antecedents,
Complex creatures make a stand.

13

Hallmarks of ancients and the more recent,
Back to the Mitochondrial Eve,
Humanity becomes its finest flower
With Consciousness as its highest power.
Complex creatures make a stand.

14

Mankind, entangled in webs of desire
For goodness, destruction and revolution,
Sets the taproot, spirituality, on fire,
Fuelling Consciousness in its evolution.
Complex creatures make a stand.

15

And we are the best evolution gets!
We would be, wouldn't we, being us!
But oh how much better we could be
Illumed in the light of mystery!
Complex creatures make a stand.

16

Complex, little universes dance
From the quantum fluctuations
To the millions of generations,
Universes that took their chance.
Complex creatures make a stand.

17

Each time enfolded seeds unfold,
The basic elements of physics
Mutate to the marvellous, rich and strange,
Out of its charmed existence
As complex creatures make a stand.

18

And some will grow like a snowdrop grows,
Some fade back in the quantum foam.
All part of a universe that breathes, survives,
And shares, reciprocates and thrives
As complex creatures make a stand.

19

Fluttering wonder is brought to life
Like the sleeping chrysalis that comes alive,
A butterfly awakened, recreated,
Taking to the air in sudden flight,
As complex creatures make a stand,

20

In the marvellous blazonry of wings
That profuse, inherited beauty brings.
O lord such wonder in every land!
Complex creatures, beautiful, grand,
Make a stand, make a stand.

21

Our Planet Earth is the nonpareil,
The child of the living cosmos.
All Life's opportunities happening
With Being itself the improbable thing
Where complex creatures make a stand.

Chapter Nine

An Exploration Of Evolution

UNIT ONE THE THEORY OF EVOLUTION

"Every great scientific truth goes through three stages. First, people say it
conflicts with the Bible. Next, they say it has been discovered before.
Lastly, they say they have always believed it."
Louis Agassiz

"What a chimera, then, is man! What a novelty, what a monster, what
a chaos, what a subject of contradiction, what a prodigy! A judge of
all things, feeble worm of the earth, depositary of the truth, cloaca of
uncertainty and error, the glory and the shame of the universe!"
Blaise Pascal

The Theory of Evolution,
Stated simply, says that Replication
Leads to random, chance Mutations
Through increased Complexification
To Natural Selection,
Not forgetting Speciation
Which requires geographical isolation.

An ancestor splits to descendent species
With independent, adaptive evolution
Like Galapogos finches' island's migrations.
Differences grow, most species go extinct,
But the history of Life is a forest of trees
Each with branching-out hierarchies.

All Life inextricably interconnected
With patterns that change and blend
Within the Absolute Consciousness,
Adaptations that never end
From the astonishing orchid flowers, to snails,
To eyes in the feathers of peacocks' tails.

They manipulate the wonder of the mystery
Of awesome beauty and simplicity,
Natural Selection creates adaptations,
That Resonate more wonderful creations,
Remodels the old in a gradual change
Into something rich and strange.

Species Consciously help the other
And by doing so, helps themselves,
As the survival of the fitter
Always makes a species better.
Nothing is ever left to chance
So the Marvellous is continually enhanced.

But no one knows how Replication arose
And Mutations form a chemical code
With increasing, complex, lettering

Of latticed crosses, while
Natural Selection, the non-random part,
Tears up the Theory in its heart.

Oh! Yes, it is a beautiful Theory,
A sight for sore eyes, dressed to kill,
Of Planet Earth's astonishing diversity
But the omission of certain Resonances
From the ever-evolving consciousnesses
Marks down the Theory as incomplete.

Even bacteria is a network of Resonances
Rather than single individual cells
That reached increased Complexification
Through chemical, genetic evolution
Though quintessentially biological!
Fast replicators push the weak to extinction.

Natural Selection steers the process
Towards a higher Longing-for-Living,
A more dynamic Consciousness.
But the core of life is still veiled here,
And the genetic, biosynthetic part
Is a broken identity belvedere.

The hard-to-read palimpsests
Are discernible as features
That evolved over slow time
From other ancestral features.
Adaptations can be staggering
In their camouflaged virtuosity.

All-Yearning-Longing-for-Survival.
What is this Life? Why? How did it start?
That's biology's crisis of identity?
The modern concept that the Laws
Of Nature defining natural phenomena
Must, they say, be merely illusory?

Not so. A Theory-of-Life
There must be,
But a theory can never quite capture
Nature's reality!

UNIT TWO AN EXAMPLE OF AN ELEMENTARY RESONANCE, CARBON CREATION AND NUCLEAR EFFICIENCY

"...And God said: Let there be Hoyle. And there was Hoyle. And God looked at Hoyle... and told him to make heavy elements in any way he pleased... but nowadays neither Hoyle, nor God, nor anyone else, can figure out exactly how it was done." Mrs George Gamow

In the beginning was the sum
Of hydrogen and helium,
Aggregated in clouds so dense
With radiation so intense,
Too hot to allow gasses to settle.

The inward tug of gravity
Against the outward expansion
Was a coincidental balance
Of exquisite precision.

But it soon began to condense
Matter in clusters and in clumps,
Until at a few million degrees
Nuclear reactions triggered,
In a process of thermonuclear fusion.

Deep in recesses, their innermost bowels,
Stars manufacture new elements.
Dense hot states in the deep starcore,
Stabilize the contraction there
As nuclei fuse in the strong nuclear force.

Nuclei that Resonate together,
Releasing double o seven per cent of their mass
As energy, in the vital essential process
To keep a star shining longer, longer.
A smaller release would demolish the Resonance.

Each element has a unique collection
Of protons, neutrons and electrons,
With a range of isotopic variations.
One proton, neutron, electron is hydrogen.
Its unique atomic number is one.

Helium two, lithium three, beryllium four,
Boron five, carbon six, nitrogen seven,
Oxygen eight, and on, on to uranium.
Positive protons repel each other
But can unite together

At high temperatures and great speeds
In nuclear transformations.
Essential in creating a strategy
For all visible reality,
For Planet Earth, for Life to be.

Carbon is three heliums joined.
Oxygen four heliums conjoined
Or a carbon plus a helium combined.
And all other elements in steps combine,
Heavier to heavier, along the line.

Will helium plus hydrogen make lithium three?
No. Won't work. Unstable you see!
Two helium nuclei make beryllium four?
No. Won't work. Shut the door!
Lithium and beryllium disintegrate at birth.

In billionths of a second, death!
No chance in this unstable state
To add a third helium so one carbon is made.
Can helium jump over lithium, beryllium,
So three heliums create carbon six?

The likelihood of such is zilch!
The logic of this? No elements.
And because of this tenuous bottleneck
No carbon-based life forms should be born.
The sequence of elements would never stand

Without a Designer's sleight-of-hand.
All elements stuck at helium! Now that's a bitch!
But hold it! We simpletons do exist!
No matter how freakish elements dance!
We are still winners! It's no game of chance!

Too small a time-span to create
Lithium, beryllium, carbon,
Nitrogen, oxygen… So no biosphere…
Stars would burn out in truncated time.
Not enough time to give us existence.

Fred Hoyle, argued that because we exist
There had to be a solution to this.
So tell us. How did carbon grow
To make silver bells and cockle shells
And Fred Hoyles all in a row?

Fred believed in Resonances.
Quantum waves in particles
Can boost a nuclear excited state
Allowing unstable beryllium prolong
Its existence so triple heliums mate

Into a single carbon cell.
In that split moment, one could Resonate
Enough to give us carbon six
While the excess energy radiates
And the nucleus settles into a ground state.

And Will Fowler found, the truth to tell,
A hundred billion billionth of a sec
Was a long enough animation spell
For the triple helium to gell.
Phew! That was close! Enough to draw sweat!

Tell me that was accidental
While I loosen my cravat!
Tell me this is just a fluke
And I'll eat my hat!
Tell me it's a Divine Dynamic,
Or some mode of Consciousness?
OK. I'll tip my hat to that!

Without that tiny Resonance,
No carbon, no Fred Hoyle!
And carbon hangs around and is stable.
It joins with helium to make oxygen.
Look at yourself! A body of carbon

Breathing gasps of oxygen!
Such infinitesimal Perfection,
Such Symmetrical interplay,
Makes the basic parameters change
Into something rich and strange.

The exact energy is absorbed and springs
Like the harmonics in violin strings.
That such properties in an atomic nucleus
Have such voltage is simply ludicrous.
But because we exist, it had to be.

Were the excited energy a tittle lower,
There would be no carbon. None would be made.
Were the oxygen energy a teeny bit higher
There would be no carbon. No life to create.
In any case there would be no water!

So stars implode and then explode
Into supernova modes
Scattering carbon, neutrino swathes
As the light of billions of stars bathe
The interstellar nurseries.

Thus stars, galaxies and life are made.
It is quite impossible this event
Could ever have happened by accident
With that awesome, awesome consequence
That the human race could then exist.

A door to welcome in you and me,
All carbon-kissing company
In a thermonuclear mystery.
Who could have done it? Tell me who
Is the clever Detective that kindled the clue?

A Mechanic who tuned the engine so fine
To keep nuclear efficiency in line.
A strange cosmological coincidence.
The hand of a Conscious Designer
Fabricating, gestating existence?

Mmmmmm...
This is just one resonance...
And there are so many more...
So many more...
Mmmmmm...

Chapter Ten

A Set of Questions Around the Big Question "What is Life?"

"The advance of scientific knowledge does not seem to make either our universe
or our inner life in it any less mysterious."
JBS Haldane
"Human nature is not created to function independently,
but in omnipresent partnership with its Maker."
Marilyn McCord Adams

QUESTION ONE. RESONANCES AND WHAT WE DESIGNATE AS LIFE?

The microfossil evidence of Life
In ancient microorganisms date
To a time billions of years ago
When cells were already on the go?
Now in the mirror I can see

Ten thousand trillion cells. That's me!
But that and a string of three billion letters
Can't capture Life's realities?

The Cell, bacterial,
A miniature factory, chemical,
Converts raw material
In synchronised reactions
Into components, functional,
With dynamic changes, continual,
To create more, more and more cells,
The substrata of all Life.

Cells, cells, cells, cells,
That hold their own integrity
Using clever, chemical energy,
Inanimate molecules
Interacting in holistic ensembles,
Interchanging Resonances,
Communities bequeathing
That which we designate as Life.

Repeatedly continual
Resonances that are chemical
And faintly biological
And Conscious and residual,
Seem to make sense
Of the trick that made existence
And enabled the continuance
Of what we designate as Life.

In Natural Selection
There has to be those Resonances
Along the spectrum of Consciousnesses
Of species, so interconnections
Create visible evidence
That impels all creatures
Towards a better existence,
Towards a designated, creative Life.

QUESTION TWO. IS IT CHEMICAL OR BIOLOGICAL?

That the ribosome molecule,
An astonishing organelle
On which all life dependence fell
Could stitch protein molecules,
Batches of amino acid molecules,
In perfect integrated assemblies,
Interconnections remarkable,
In nearly no time at all
Is virtually inconceivable!

This organised complexity contradicts
The Second Law of Thermodynamics?
Physics and biology are incompatible!
Biology undermines the physics law
As cells become more orderly,
Leaving biologists in awe
Since nature always increases entropy?

Nature does not design spontaneously
With deliberate intent any organised entity.
So we have a biological problem
That could never happen by chance.!
And the Theory of Evolution
Lights on a chemical solution?
Does that make it one of the also-rans?

How could inanimate, lifeless matter
Be transformed into simple life,
Come alive, create and sing and dance
And organise increased complexity,
Nature's staggering diversity,
With spectacular creativity
By some nebulous, random chance?

QUESTION THREE. WHAT ARE THE CHANCES
FOR LIFE?

How could a primitive batch
Of inanimate materials hatch
The golden egg that came alive
Or did some magical Hen lay that surprise?

Or could it be this
Astonishing design
Was dreamed up in
An infinite, Conscious Mind?

Or do organisms'
Patterns glow,

Like photons from
An electromagnetic flow?

What could explain
The chemical transformation,
Travelling life's road
Down a biological direction?

And why would inanimate matter open
The biological gate
In a planet, entirely inhospitable
In its prebiotic state?

The chances the right amino acids will fall
Into an enzyme are so small
That you may say with all sincerity
It couldn't happen at all, at all!

And when you imagine
How you came to be
That indefinity seems to be
Closer to an infinite improbability!

QUESTION FOUR REPLICATING RESONANCES AND CONSCIOUSNESS

As to when the replicator rose
We have absence of evidence
Or how the metabolism grows
Shows evidence of absence?

Was it a vague, improbable chance
Or some clear cosmic imperative
That Life stepped out in the floral dance
In its designed definitive?

The simplest of beginnings, bacteria,
Are a network of Resonances,
Stirrings of a slow, slow Longing-to-Be,
Aware of its fellow presences?

As evolution proceeded along time's path
So did levels of Consciousness
Resonate, transcend and choreograph
Higher levels of meaning and awareness,

From the particle to the single cell
To the sentient body, to the soul,
To the high reaches of reflection,
All aspects of the undivided Whole,

All enwrapped in the Collective Conscious,
Unfolding, enfolding and unfolding
As all life strained in Longing-to-Reach
Its own transcendent knowing.

Look in the mirror. What do you see?
Ten thousand trillion cells. You! Me!
Can a string of three billion letters
Capture our human reality?

For all we can say, human destiny
Rises above and beyond those cells
To unconditional charities,
Symbolic languages, symphonies,
Beauty, poetry, drama, dance
With a mind to liberate, to understand
The wonder of all that makes us be.

QUESTION FIVE RANDOM OR WHAT?

"Applying molecular genetics to questions of early human population
history, and hence
to major issues in prehistoric archaeology, is becoming so fruitful an
enterprise
that a new discipline—archaeogenetics—has recently come into
being." Colin Renfrew

In the Theory of Evolution
Innumerable mutations
Create near infinite varieties
Of spectacular species
In tundra, in deserts, in forests, in seas,
In gardens, in caverns, in tropics, in trees
As time goes slowly by.

Each random, chance mutation
Is absolutely
Independent, yet each functions
Collectively
In a seemingly ordered way.
Each chance event defines a law,
Yet all together they create a law?

So creation, reason and orderliness
Are based on consummate randomness?
This cannot be so.
Each fundamental particle knows
Where every other particle goes,
Is aware, is informed, is kith and kin
Of the Wholeness it participates in.

What seems to us as random
Is a Continuum of Resonances
In a Conscious universe
And the subtlest differences
Are creative similarities
In ever-changing categories
That always lead to orderliness.

The science of chaos tells us
That chaos is enfolded
Behind a façade of order
And reality is attained through sequences
Of orderly significances.
There is no such thing as random
In the Theory of Evolution.

Nothing is ever left to chance,
No separation possible
Between the dancer and the dance.
The element of Consciousness
Pervades this extraordinary process.

QUESTION SIX DO SOME GENES GET SMARTER?

"A man must have a certain amount of intelligent ignorance to get anywhere."
Charles Kettering
"How come dumb stuff seems so smart while you're doing it?"
Denis the Menace

DNA transmits genetic properties
Yet has chemical possibilities
That patrol along the sequences,
Searching out errors, making corrections,

But rare changes left uncorrected
Become fixed in the material,
A pool of genetic variation
Allowing natural selection.

Accuracy was essential for fidelity
Within the genetic archive.
The odd mistake too in transcription
Was essential to provide

The raw variation
To enable organisms to adapt.
Differences between giraffes and cats,
Dodos, kingfishers, zebras and bats

Lay in the digital patterns,
In the long strings of four chemicals
Whose secrets had been veiled
Over thousands, millions of years.

But how did the mechanism work
By which a living thing could construct?
A gene can generate a catalogue
Of widely different proteins

And modified protein versions
That grow more and more complex.
Oh! Yes. The genes gets smarter
And the proteins even smarterer-

Say vertebrates smarter than bacteria-
With higher levels of Awareness
In their behavioural repertoire,
Knowing, knowing where there at!

Better able to respond to nuances
In the chemical cytoplasm around cells
With greater environmental Awareness.
In other words, Consciousness.

A biological Consciousness!
Various sequences switch genes on
With a discrete element of intelligence
Knowing the compass of the gene's influence.

A repertoire of genetic information
Can generate immense concentrations,
Say, within the human brain,
Which transcends the biological substrate

Until Consciousness on the higher plane
Creates poetry, art and mathematics,
Artifacts, judicious and aesthetic,
Monuments to the unaging intellect.

All biochemical phenomena
Had an original unity
In the magnificent principles
Of simplicity and beauty.

QUESTION SEVEN WHY IS HUMAN DNA MOSTLY JUNK?

"There lives the dearest freshness deep down things."
G.M. Hopkins
"Life is perhaps the only riddle that we shrink from giving up."
William Gilbert

Human DNA is mostly junk!
Oh! The virtuosity of junk
Whose sequences are non-random!
A place where lovely somethings lurk.

While little sequences called microsatellites
Can cause cancerous mutations
Or create from an inedible weed,
Maize, full of oil, starch, protein

And other strange innovations,
Multiple genetic modifications,
Little changes constellations,
Stranger mysteries

Are not encoded in the genes
Like Fibonacci series in some plants!
Or the weird morphology
Of each six-cornered snowflake!

Or a beetle's inverse correlation
Between horn and eye size!
Or creatures with either special eyesight
Or sense of smell but never both!

Or dogs that are all colour blind
But whose sense of smell can lead the blind!
Or butterfly wings the right size
For when they are set for sudden flight!

Or athletes who know the usefulness
Of the bronchial tree's geometry
That allows air to flow in alveoli
To maximise lungs efficiency!

For us humans, billions of neurons,
Interconnected, interpenetrated,
Exist in the human brain
Yet the evolution of languages,

The redeeming power of faith
And thought are on another plane
And transcend genetic constraints
And in this place the role of genes

Is next to impossible to explain.
Just call it Human Consciousness.

QUESTION EIGHT WHAT IS THE ORIGIN OF SPECIES?

Life procreates in its different ways,
Spontaneously self-organising,
Self-replicating everywhere,
The way each six-cornered snowflake drifts,

Softly, from the dust of Antarctic mists.
From generation to generation,
Inheritance, camouflage, variation,
Colour and speed and adaptation

Of all that's weird and wonderful
To amplify diversity
And bring to finely tuned perfection
The irreducible complexity

Of evolutionary selection,
Lurk in the brightest, darkest corners,
And breathes fire into procreation
And small mutations make massive changes.

Duplicate genes, a man and a mouse!
Would a little tinkering with the genome
Change the code that I espouse?
As the missus says "Are you a man or mouse?"

All truth is female!
Ouch! Ouch! Ouch!
Take this incredible Cosmic Designer.
No blinking, tinkering part- timer.

The Giver and the Taker, the Ultimate Artificer,
The precision Watchmaker.
The appliance of the beauty of modern science,
Its catastrophes and its triumphs,

Dilute and squelch, lay waste and smash,
Squash and squelch, quosh and plash,
The sweet ancestral sense of awe,
Lost for all posterity

As Time's impending demise
Moves towards darkness and empty space.
So what is the origin of species?
A fossil record of histories?

Evolution is slow, is slow, is slow.
Or else it is quick, is quick, is quick.
Stasis with bursts of inflation show
It is incomplete, it is incomplete.

We still don't know,
We still don't know.
And Darwin's Tree of Life,
The gradual accumulation

Of small hereditary fine tuning
Would seem to be a no, no, no.
Australia, cut off for untold aeons,
Has idiosyncratic marsupials, moles,

That look like American placented ones
And the camera eyes' complexities
Share similar parts independently
And crocodiles along the Nile

Are fifty million years of age,
Trapped in an evolutionary cul-de-sac
And dragonflies who first took flight
Two hundred million years ago

Are the same dragonfly dinners
Gobbled by recent birds and web spinners?
Such astonishing design directions
As all grope towards more complexity,

Were inbuilt in the original intention,
With life-forms stretched for durability,
All evidence of a skillful Designer,
A Conscious, Absolute Substantiality.

QUESTION NINE IS THERE A COSMIC IMPERATIVE?

If you want to tell God a good joke, tell Him your plans for the future.
A joke!!!
"Forgive, O Lord, my little jokes on Thee,
And I'll forgive Thy great big one on me."
Robert Frost

Evolution moves at its own sweet pace.
Cells reflect the miraculous,

With turbines, motors
Propellers and rotors,
Efficient, networking and autonomous.

Cells that photosynthesise light,
Co-operate to evolve and survive
And Resonate co-instantaneously
And simultaneously
In the creativity of new life.

Organic life, that rare phenomenon,
Seeming to thrive on chains of chance,
Is more a cosmic inevitability,
Where it is, it will, evolve, to be,
Unravelling genetic mysteries.

Atoms and molecules meld into cells
Of greater Conscious intent,
More fulfilment, experience,
Subtler forms of significance,
Along a Spectrum of Consciousness.

As evolution proceeds, all spectrum levels
Resonate, transcend and choreograph
Towards higher meanings, from particle,
The protointelligence, to matter, to sentient,
To subtle, to soul and mystical transcendence.

Each species pre-cognitively aware
Of changes in its Longing-To-Be.
More complex physical forms evolve

From simpler cellular one
Through conscious evolution and change.

Evolution is the movement of the universe
Towards its own coherence,
Towards higher states of subtlety.
Beings imprint their own significance
In the parish where they settle

And extend creative possibilities
Within their real personal presence,
Increasing the bank of all reality.
Consciousness always was and will be
Whatever the conditions of Life seem to be.

So on ad infinitum as each cell organises
Subtler forms of Significances
Longing to reach a higher state,
The absolute,
Mystical Transcendences,

Modulators of these mysteries,
All alive intoxicatingly
In All-There-Is in landscape, seascape,
Skyscape and mindscape.
Oh! Life is the cosmic imperative!

All in a self-regulating craft,
With an Omniscient Omnipotent
Arranging the drifting rubble,
The inscrutable bubble,
Taking charge of the thermostat,

With interstellar panspermia,
Under the chorus of gravity,
Seeding Creation's entities,
Playing the planetary orchestra,
Creating, sustaining the operas of life.

Still physicists will demur, cry there is no design,
Because science is a dog scratching for bones,
Reaching for tentatives, the unknowns,
While faith draws mankind nearer the Divine
Whose wheels are subtle, exceedingly fine.

Chapter Eleven

Home Thoughts to Mull Over

UNIT ONE CREATION AND EVOLUTION.

The secrets of evolution
Are death and time.

Time for the slow accumulation
Of patterns of favourable mutations
And all creatures are butterflies
Who flutter for a day and think it is forever.
Even Man is but a mayfly
Briefly, tenuously flickering
In this strangely, beautiful place,
This astonishingly, creative space.

And yet when all is said and done,
The hummingbird needled his beak, his tongue,
And fused the rhythms of his wings.
The kestrel, scanning from the peak,

Saw shadows shifting in lakes, fields.
The shark perfected his fins, his teeth.
The eye evolved to use the light.
Earth avails of the Sun's white light.

Beatles have the greatest diversity,
Adapting in terrestrial niches.
The gentlest butterflies and bees
Pollinate flowers to enrich us.
We sift reality to feel the awe.
Yet the beauty of the red, red rose
From which the honeyed fragrances flow
Won't from electrochemicals grow.

The sequences of the existence
Of selected processes in the universe
Are undeniable evidence
Of life's supreme opportunism.
We take what's there without a thought
And stitch ourselves into its cloth.
We wear that fabric, audaciously woven,
From mysteries tentatively proven.

Every oak seed longs to be a tree,
A kingfisher egg to fly,
And salmon climb up waterfall rocks
Back to their home to breed and die.
All things aspire to persevere
In their own essential Being,
All Conscious to a certain degree
Of their virtual Potentiality.

Creation is some enchanted state,
From the howling reaches of outer space
Steeped in the marvels, mysteries of fate,
That evolved Planet Earth and the human race.

UNIT TWO WHAT IS IT GAVE US OUR HUMANNESS?

"To err is human, to forgive divine."
Alexander Pope
"For a novelist, a given historic situation is an anthropologic laboratory in which he explores his basic question: What is human existence?"
Milan Kundera

All life is linked by a common syllabus
Written in a chemical code, DNA,
An archive of parts of living things,
And genes in energy production,
Housed in organelles
Inside the living cells
From which genetic material is composed.

This code of long sequences
Of four "letters", C, T, G and A
Strung out in different combinations
And in combined differences
Like multi-coloured beads in a necklace.
The information of DNA is encoded
In the precise order these four go.

Each sequence has a unique story,
The relentless pilgrimage through time,
Life's history back to its embryo,
And while most phenomena leave no trace,
Melting like six cornered snowflakes,
Living things keep a tiny instruction
Of their operation, their construction,
In the miniature archive of DNA.

So matter, energy and Consciousness
Are creations of All-There-Is.
What opening gambit in this game of chess
Began the Spectrum of Consciousness
Which sponsors all creativity,
The metaphysical Longing-To-Be
That permeates all our reality
At all times instantaneously?

God, the Divine, or call it what you will
Is the Absolute Consciousness
Suffuse with all-knowing presences,
A living atmosphere that exists,
Invisible, explicating the real,
Permeating All-There-Is
From which springs all existences
Along the spectrum of Consciousness,

From the bacterium to the mystical state,
Each with a Consciousness of its own kind,
Each intermeshed and intimate with
And interpenetrated in the Absolute.

All-There-Is breathes Consciousness.
All energy is Eternal, a Continuum,
Aware of what it Long-To-Become
Through its innate, imbued creativity

And humankind is the transcendent,
The pink of Conscious perfection.
All-There-Is speaks softly, softly to us
Through its timeless, timeless Consciousness
That wallows, wallows in creativity
And faith brings wonder, wonder and fulfilment
In our Conscious, Conscious environment,
Full of sustenance and spontaneity.

UNIT THREE DIVINE DESIGN

"The world that science describes seems to me, with its order,
intelligibility,
potentiality, and tightly knit character, to be one that is consonant
with the idea
that it is the expression of the will of a Creator."
John Polkinghorne.
"God is the perfect poet,
Who in his person acts his own creation."
Robert Browning

All life participates in time
And living things are shapes in space
Out of a haven of timelessness
In an eternal, ineffable place.

Vibrations of thought within this space
Create time, create the universe,
While matter gives it a visible shape,
Vibrations from the silences.

At this open door we can look and see
The world of time, of eternity,
A rainbow cosmos that illuminates itself
In the self-replicating prism eternally.

Science alone cannot adjudicate
On the Divine Design hypothesis,
Nor invent either the presumption
That faith does or does not exist,

Nor dogmatise on transcendence
With intelligent integrity,
Nor wallow in the need for evidence
To bolster scientific legitimacy,

Nor marginalise the Divine Design
Over aeons of time in weird mutations
With accidental, natural selections,
Governed by chance and random selections

With its pitiless indifference,
For the beauty, the wonder, that Nature is.
Could it be the astonishing diversity, disparity,
Is the wisdom of God's Creativity.

UNIT FOUR SCIENCE VS. THEOLOGY.

"God reveals Himself through Nature, so to study Nature is to study God."
Thomas Aquinas
"One of the disabling weaknesses of current western literature is its unwillingness or inability to engage with the dance of the spirit in the sciences."
George Steiner

In the vanity fair of ideologies,
Physicists obsessed with the physical,
The mathematical, the theoretical,
Lose sight of the transcendental.
The deeper significance of the real
Is the blind spot of the irrational.

Science is enquiry. Theology is faith.
Aspects that are rational or spiritual wraiths.
Science is a dog scratching for a bone,
Reaching for the tentative, the unknown.
In faith mankind is nearer the Divine
Whose wheels are subtle and ever fine.

This Universe pregnant with all sorts of life
Seeding the inevitability,
As though its life-soul had a plan,
That predicated the arrival of Man,
And his irreducible complexity.
No miracles, more out of necessity.

Together with Nature's subtlety,
Elegance, simplicity and diversity,
Harmonious cleverality,
Unfathomable niceties,
All is one dense landscape of possibilities,
Stemming from Transcendence,

Which upholds Existence,
In every place, at every moment.
It lets it get on with its intent.
The universe conspires for you and me.
It radiates the beauty that we see
And love is its highest frequency.

Unwavering faith in the Unseen,
As the journey through life unfolds,
Is the headlights that reveal the road before
To bring us safe through the dark night home.
Evolution sings with a million voices
Making bizarre and beautiful choices.

These reflect a deeper reality
In its astonishing creativity.
The newness in every stale thing
Wells up inside invisibly, silently,
And transcends the waking state
Spontaneously,

As it creeps towards its potential,
Towards self-communing,
Towards an interior belvedere,

An imperceptible enlightening,
The kind of Consciousness
That meditative knowing brings.

As reality moves like an ocean wave
We catch the reflection in the cave.
Faith must not compete with science,
Its fundamental certainties
But keep the spotlight on the mystical,
The transcendental mysteries.

Science can never uncreate
What a Supernatural Creator made
No more than religion would invalidate
The physical laws that testify
To the timeless biofriendliness
Of our planet Earth and our Universe.

Mystics, the Einsteins of Consciousness,
Grapple with fine, divine realities,
Unattainable, mystical mysteries,
That pour out of Its Ineffable Mind.
And faith itself is never blind,
A Providential-Work-In-Progress.

Scientists with a mish-mash of mathematics
And bewildering abstractions
Unravel parts of the cosmic physics,
With brilliant, profound, astounding tricks,
Forever doomed to be incomplete,
Logic imprisoned in a jail of flaws

With the Godhead a disappearing wraith.
But they too have the greatest faith
In the unity of all that nature creates,
And peer into the Consciousness to see
Nature's awesome, eternal beauty,
Shadows of sheer Authenticity.

Time for the scientist, the theologian,
To break sacramental bread in peace,
Sit at table together and feast
On the wonder of our experience,
On the heavens, images of the divine,
From luminous galaxies that rip and burn,

To elusive electrons that twirl and turn,
All shadows of the eternal light,
Rainbows woven with wondrous delight,
From unknowable quivering superstrings,
To the flutterings of angels' wings,
All rational and all intangible things.

Chapter Twelve

A Musical Interlude, The Song Of The Materialists

"If you accept unqualified materialism you are forced to question the existence of free will, deny any notion of spiritual truth and abandon hope of transcendence."
Rita Carter
"It's presumptuous to tell someone else why she believes what she believes—if you want to know, start by asking her."
Louise Anthony

Come all you lumbering robots
And listen unto me,
Don't side with any theorists
Till you know what their theory be,
Evolutionary ideology decrees
Matter the one and only reality,
But this scientific creed is in
A crisis of crumbling credibility.

These materialists, believe you me,
Say things are all mechanical.
Matter unconscious and purposeless,
Inheritance all biological.
An ideal Marxist world, reflected by the mind,
Of a material existence, its evolution,
All in a state of flux, interacting,
In dramatic transformations.

Inexplicable phenomena are illusory,
The mind a physics thing in your head,
The laws of nature are fixed in life
And your memories obliterated when you're dead.
Memories are in the brain.
The brain decays at death.
What better proof for atheists
Of the folly of religious faith?

Evolution is the random
Chance mutation of genes.
Replay the tape of Life and I
Might be a beetle or a string of beans!
How could spontaneous variation
And natural selection evolve mankind,
Its creativity, its intellect,
Knowing Fortuna is always blind?

Natural Selection, the non-random part,
More a definitive choice,
Born from bacterial Consciousness
To higher, more transcendent levels,

That harmonise, resonate, voice-on-voice,
Echoing interconnectedness
As each is aware of all others growing
And existence multiplies in this knowing.

The Longing-for- Life could no longer wait
And all Is-Still-Longing to this day.
Existence thrives and survives
In this mutual, reciprocal, toing-and-froing.
We think, therefore we are, the real deal!
And we have reached the mountain-top!
Oh! Life is wonderfully real.
I know that I know. So let's get going!

The molecular biology of atoms,
Smashed, evanescent, particle showers,
Could never reflect the beauty
Of the aura around an orchid flower.
Methinks the materialists have issued a wad
Of promissory notes as truths,
All devalued by their omniscience,
By hyperinflation and their own taboos.

Spontaneous things like weather and waves
Are simply unpredictable.
Even with their diamond, planetary motion,
Certainty is unachievable.
All their scientific, omniscient doctrines
Have been shattered to smithereens
By Quantum, by Relativity,
By the Big Bang and expanding galaxies.

The magisterium of soulless science,
With its accidental atomic collisions,
Drifts in the bleak expanding debris
Where its destiny is extinction.
And all the works of days and hands,
Monuments to man's intellect, flair,
Are rubbled away to meaninglessness,
To hopelessness and despair.

Those material evangelists find
Salvation in social reform of late.
But wait! Their belief in humanity
Proves theirs too is a matter of faith.
Science modelled on a paradigm
Of questions, answers, anomalies,
Leads on to crises, to answers, to facts,
And to newly invented mysteries.

Scientists, prisoners of their own prenotions,
In caves of shadows, of taboos,
Must break out into the light,
Grasp phenomena without further ado,
For DNA molecules are intelligent,
They move in mysterious ways
And aspire to Immortality
And always know which cards to play.

The visible universe is four per cent.
That's one of Einstein's tricks.
Is there a physicist who can tell me
About the other ninety-six?

Dark Matter and Dark Energy
Have physics in a hypothetical spin!
Conservation Laws will never hold
Unless Dark Energy is ignored!
And Dark Matter is annihilated
Or slowly grows exceedingly thin!

Our planet is the one, the only one
With exact, anthropic conditions.
Could any physicist perfect the maths
To make another that one in a zillion?
Energy, elusive, breathes life in it,
Change underpinned by mystery,
The Indestructible, the Immutable,
And atoms indestructible.

The girl in the red carnation dress
Is a basket of atoms that follow rules,
But the beauty of her flowing stroll
Is more than the sum of her molecules!
Out in the quantum vacuum field,
The jewel of quantum predictions,
Particles appear and disappear,
Throbbing with hypothetical interactions.

Between the transcendent and material
Lies the Nous, beyond comprehending,
And how the laws, the constants, were imprinted
Is all beyond our understanding.
Could the evolution of flora and fauna
Like the background radiation release,

Be applied to chemical elements
And an evolutionary Universe?

Could patterns inherited from the past,
Resonate across time and space?
All drawn from a collective memory,
Creativity enfolding every place.
What is the source of creativity
That spontaneously life enacts
Through portals of infinite richness,
Where intellect is but one aspect?

If matter is the only reality
Consciousness aught not be.
It does. Am I merely molecules?
Yes. But much more. I am Me.
And each thing that exists will strive
To persevere in its essence, its being.
And Consciousness is the Being-There,
Quantum sentient energy becoming.

The past drifts into the present now
Out of an inexhaustible source,
The future is the chosen potentials
In the Now, conditioned by what occurs.
Consciousness forces molecular complexes
To make inherent choices
So all things are Conscious in their way,
Not improbable, random voices.

All ends strain to a definite future,
A seedling longs to be a flower,
The salmon finds its spawning ground,
The egg awaits its breaking hour.
The latent forces of creativity
Like languages, insights and innovations,
Were divine purposeful evolutions,
Not natural laws and chance mutations.

Phenomena are not explicable
In the guise of microscopic bubbles
And the sacramental sanctity
Evaporates in a chapel's rubble.
Shored where scientific progress bends,
Evolution splits nature and humanity,
Materialist science with human ends
Triumphing in a catastrophic destiny.

Consciousness nestles in the matrix
Of a cosmic evolutionary process
Which draws all life through inheritance
To patterns of morphic Resonance.
Our memories do not decay
But resound by resonant flight
In the collective memory of species
Out of a vast ocean of mystical light.

Come all you transcendent humans
And put your faith in me.
Don't side with any theorist
Till you know the wood for the trees.

Don't side with the materialists
From the dark night till the noon
Or you will find your certainties
To be wired up to the moon.

Chapter Thirteen

The Copenhagen Interpretation

*"Those who are not shocked when they first come across
quantum theory cannot possibly understand it."*
Niels Bohr

*"Bohr is like a sensitive child and walks about this world in a kind of
hypnosis. Seldom in my life has a person given me such pleasure by his
mere presence."*
Albert Einstein

UNIT ONE NIELS BOHR (1885-1962)

Along came the incredible Bohr,
Who softly opened the quantum door.
Niels, brilliant, smiling, refined,
The Golden Dane, patient and kind.
Lover of football, cowboys, the Wild West,

With a razzledazzle of luminaries,
He sailed across infinitesimal seas

To usher in the Age of Discoveries:
Such as infinite space, nanotechnology,
Petscans, predicating Dark Energy,

Internet, medical creative zones,
Lazers, I T, portable phones,
Computers, why the warm Sun shines,
Nuclear reactors, digital signs
And a million other things, most yet unknown,
Such as the ghost inside the atom
And the tackle gears of Consciousness.

UNIT TWO THE PRINCIPLE OF COMPLEMENTARITY

Nature is inherently unknowable.
The particle/wave sides of matter and light
Are two faces of the same phenomenon,
And the system's final behaviour is set
By the act of observation.

The paradox of wave-particle duality?
How to reconcile these mutually exclusives?
Bohr came up with Complementarity
For these civil indispensables.

Photons paint one picture of light.
The wave aspect paints another.
Both facets of one phenomenon.
On opposite walls yet side by side?

You can observe only one at a time.
Light will behave the way it will
Depending on the choice of experiment
And the act of observation.

Electrons can take up residence only
In orbits that accord with energy levels.
Give them a kick and they jump up
To a higher-energy, orbital state.

Later they fall back down to ground state
And give off a photon with delight,
Emitting a different coloured light,
Like red, yellow, green, blue or violet.

Electrons shuffle up and down,
Absorbing or emitting photons,
Forming a pattern of spectral lines,
Each line accords with a singular jump.

Different elements, different spectra,
Distinctive radiation fingerprints,
Unique for each chemical element
And like the supermarket's code of bars

They reveal the composition of the stars,
And invisible atoms we can see
Through the use of spectroscopy.
Electrons that in elliptical, circular shells,

Around in stationary, whirling wheel,
Can instantaneously disappear
And in another shell reappear
In orbits out from the nucleus, higher.

Such animated intricacy!
Breath-taking diversity!
Spectacular creativity!
The quantum world's efficiency!

Is this a romantic, picturesque love-affair
In an idealised, fictional atmosphere?
Or could this be a fundamental process
Of some ineffable Consciousness?

UNIT THREE THE WAVE FUNCTION COLLAPSE

Matter and energy are equivalent
And inter-convertible.
Matter associated with a wave
Which is virtually undetectable.

When an observation or measurement is made,
One of the electron's possible states
Becomes its actual state.
The probability of other possibilities becomes zero.

Enigmatic, exclusive, and indispensable.
By a maths formulation, only, measurable.
It is connected to us intimately. Intimately.
We know it as the Wave Function.

The wave –particle duality is a strange reality.
Measure position-momentum, the wave will collapse.
Measuring one precludes the other.
Mutually exclusive yet complimentary.

They coexist yet are seemingly incompatible
And when they change it can be irrevocable.
All possible quantum states exist potentially,
Each with a probability to exist in our reality.

Reality enacted by the act of observation.
One choice from a myriad. A Metaphysical act.
With that act, the real is made manifest
And each time the Wave Function will collapse.

So an electron, in its Potential sense,
Unperceived, shooting around the atom
In ever widening circular wheels
Is actually nowhere, until observed!

Then the spectrum of waveforms becomes zero bar one
Which designates the point of measurement.
The Wave Function, a series of probability states,
Collapses instantaneously to a point.

What is the site of the Wave Function Collapse?
From quantum ghost to real existence?
And how is observation defined?
Eugene Wigner was bothered by this enigma.

Is it the sideways glance of a mouse
Or the moony blink of a frog
Or the happy-go-lucky wink of a louse
Or can the electron itself do the job?

Or could the Quantum Potential, non-local,
Superliminal, Whole, underlying Hidden Domain,
Guide the travelling particle
To explicate the electron.

Or could the electron's Consciousness
Create its own explication,
Despite quantum indeterminacy
And the lack of it in ours?

All part of the Spectrum of Consciousness
In a world that is quantum mechanical.
The Wave Function is collapsed by vigilance
In a world that exists in potential.

Quantum reinstates the Mystical into physics.
Abstractions that contradict everyday experience.
A state of Possibilities with unseen probabilities
Unfold into our three-dimensional world.

From a timeless domain we make infinite choices,
From an illimitable reservoir of Light, of Consciousness.
The Quantum World, interconnectedly Whole,
Has an interpenetratedly, intermeshed Soul.

Along the Spectrum of Consciousness,
Presences surround and engulf us.
We are part of this magical web because
Elementaries can behave as particles\waves.

They are Potentialities. This Consciousness
Is a phenomenon of complex, non-conscious neurons.
I know that you are really you
But yet I cannot prove it true!

The Wave Function for a beam of light
Contains all possibilities within it
Whether appearing in wave or particle guise
But only in one form when you measure it!

Each physical form interprets here
In an all-inclusive atmosphere
According to its Desire-for-Being
Out of the Wave Function Domain.

Our Mind determines which.
An indefinite reality. Not what you see.
When atomic, unstable particles decay
You can predict the probability.

Neils Bohr's universe is probabilistic.
But the electrons themselves well know
Where they are going to go,
And know where all other electrons go

Like a million sardines in a rounded shoal,
Each sardine knowing the right way to roll
Or murmurations of starlings that rise and fall
In an instantaneous, synchronised puffball.

UNIT FOUR MAX BORN. (1882-1970), THE PROBABILITY INTERPRETATION OF THE WAVE FUNCTION

"Nothing is certain with the wave. Mere possibilities in a ground state."
Max Born

Max Born in the summer of 1926
Found inconsistencies that fell
Out of experiments where nothing would gell.
A theory based on observables!

Why speak of invisible electron paths
Inside invisible atom tracks?
He found a way to reconcile particles and waves
And found that the square of the Wave Function

Turned out to be a physical probability
Of the associated particle's presence,
A quantum state's real existence,
But its probability is all we can know.

One can only speak of the Probability
Of where the particle will be observed.
The Probability is
Where the energy packet might be.

Apply the equation.
Find the solution.
It is the Wave Function.
In space. Over time. Moves the electron.

Chapter Fourteen

The Meeting Of Great Minds

UNIT ONE THE NATURE OF THE QUANTUM SOUL: NIELS BOHR VS. ALBERT EINSTEIN

"The ultimate success will never be ours. Nowhere in the castle of
science is there a final exit to the absolute truth."
Rudy Rucker

On the nature of wave/particle duality
Niels Bohr brought together all he could see
And found a system clearly undefined
With the potential of possibilities.

So wave and particle properties,
Must seem as Complementarities.

Waves or particles of sunlight fall
Like paintings hanging on opposite walls.
Look at one. Turn. Look at the other.
Each exclusive, but mutually together.

In the Copenhagen Interpretation,
Bohr claimed the answer to the question,
"In Nature's mutually exclusive game,
Is light a particle or is light a wave?"

It simply depends on the question asked
Or the kind of experiment one may enact.
The measuring makes it actual
And the observation makes it real.

Einstein dismissed the probabilities.
The path is only temporary.
Thought experiments, probability,
Quantum mechanics and uncertainty.

In September 1927, in Como's lakeside
Bohr detailed his Principle of Complementarity
Far from the critical ear of Einstein
Who refused to set foot on fascist Italy.

What was at stake between Einstein and Bohr
Was the nature of the Quantum Soul.
Does Science seek to reveal the real
Or its probabilities reveal?

UNIT TWO THE SOLVEY CONFERENCE, OCTOBER 1927

"At the Solvey Conference on "Photons and Electrons" in 1927, the most spectacular meeting-of-minds ever was held. The confusion of ideas reached its zenith."
Paul Langevin

Whatever the future in space and time,
The quantum theory stands sublime.
Hendrik Lorentz, the Dutch Grandmaster,
In October, nineteen twenty-seven,

Sent out letters to those that mattered,
The classical physicists and their betters.
Twenty-nine maestros came to Solvey
To discuss, to assess, reassess and to pray.

So all week long the quantum battle rolled,
On the nature of Reality—Einstein v Bohr.
No more than Tantalus, parched with thirst,
Could drink the water that bobbed at his chin

Or bite a lump of the vanishing fruit,
Both men longed for the elusive Truth.
Come on Albert. Face the Truth!
Niels. We are not too sure you will win!

Bohr, his matrices, Heisenberg, Pauli,
Preachers of particles, Discontinuity,
Uncertainty, Complimentarity,
Abstract Reality a probability.

Einstein, Schrodinger and de Broglie,
Quantum waves and Continuity.
A simpler three-dimensional place,
Where what is, exists, in Time and Space.

And Georges Lamaitre too had his day,
Reminding Albert in his way,
"You're equations of General Relativity
Require more dramatic scrutiny.

The Creation story we must rewrite.
Your Cosmological Constant is not right.
You cannot ignore what is in the maths.
Come on Albert. Face the Facts!

All once was a mote of immensest density
That would stretch even your imagination,
A primeval atom, swelled in time,
In a universe driven by expansion."

To what seemed an affront, Einstein replied,
"Your reverend mathematics,
Correct though they may seem to be,
But make no mistake your physics

Are simply abhorrent to me.
The universe is unchanging. It is fixed.
I will not bow to a mathematician's will.
It's not expanding and it never will!"

UNIT THREE A GAME OF CHESS

*"He called me a fatalist, but I'd never collected a postage stamp in
my life."*
Yogi Berra

They all sat down to a game of Chess.
The prize? Reality's soul. Nothing less.
The king listened to this and that.
On evenings sprung rabbits from his hat.

The Danish queen gathered round her chicks.
These pawns admired her little tricks.
The castle, banished out of town,
Wistfully drew the portcullis down.

The silent knight, riding on high,
Bemused, observed, kept his powder dry.
The rooks, deferential, seen and unseen,
Took oaths of allegiance to the queen.

The queen attacked in increasing violence,
Stunning the deferential king to silence,
Until she, clutching the crown to her breast,
Cried, "Checkmate", to the hapless king.

The queen had won the game of Chess.
But-maybe-only-for-the-time-being or less?
When the meeting ended, the pawn and queen
Were locked away in the same box

And all the greatest minds there were,
All the most brilliant minds of the day
Went along on their merry way
Back to their institutes.

Still the little electrons laughed and spun
Near the speed of light,
They would whirl and turn
In a quantum dance of perpetual fun.

UNIT FOUR A THEORY OF EVERYTHING

"Nothing is more interesting than nothing, nothing is more puzzling
than nothing
and nothing is more important than nothing."
Ian Stuart

Einstein went to search for a unified theory
That he believed would save causality
And an observer-independent reality.
A complete unified field, a TOE.

Later in the States, heard Lamaitre's maths
That proved the first primordial flash
Burst outwards into swelling space
Whose burning embers were the embryos
Of all the stars and galaxies we know.

This time Einstein was more impressed.
He warmly complimented the priest.
"This is a most beautiful explanation
Of the first moments of Creation."

But still he demurred and contradicted
Heisenberg's Probability Law.
Bohr stood his ground and refuted,
Teasing out each miscalculation, each flaw.

Einstein showed Bohr a gallows light-box
With a hole, a shutter, a measure, a clock,
In a thought experiment, if you please.
A photon released, some energy lost.

Now measure the change, reweigh the box!
The theory must be incomplete!
As the shutter opens, the photon's released.
For Bohr the photon source will recoil

Causing uncertainty in place and time.
Gravity changes the flow of Time!!!
Einstein was hoist on his own theory
Of General Relativity!!!

Einstein undone. Mechanics. Uncertainty.
Still. A niggle irked his mirage of reality.
Then along came Schrodinger with a cat
Which he flung among the pigeons.

UNIT FIVE SCHRODINGER'S CAT

"If this is the Captain, I'm gonna have a word with him. My hot water's been cold for three days. And I haven't got enough room to swing a cat. In fact I haven't got a cat."
Groucho Marx in "Monkey Business."
"In Schrodinger's Equation, the wave tells the particle where to go, the particle tells the wave where to start and stop".
Alfred S. Goldhaber

The hardest thing of all is to see
A black cat in a darkened larder.

But if in the larder there is no cat,
Then the job is even harder, harder.

Erwin Schrodinger had found the equation,
The maths engine for Quantum Mechanics.
It dictates how a probability wave
Evolves in time, evolves in time,
And the mathematical embodiment of the whole
Is the sum of all its parts, its parts.

But his beautiful equation did, it did,
Over time stagnate,
Over time stagnate,
So he created a "thought-experiment" because
It would show how absurd wave measurement was.

Schrodinger had the idea that
There once was a purring cat,
A puss-in-boots,
With a grin, a sword and swashbuckling boots,
Locked in a sealed, a metal box,
With a hammer, a Geiger counter and a clock,

And a flask of hydro-cyanide.
Holy God! Hydro cyanide!
Enough to ensure the pussycat died.
And a radioactive atom on a tray
With a fifty-fifty-possibility it may,
Or may not, in one exact hour decay.

If the radioactive atom decays
It triggers the hammer
That smashes the flask
That releases the gas
Whose nebulousness
Simply kills the cat.

And the cat will be dead as a cat can be,
A cat as dead as a lump of lead,
And the mouses all can come out to play
The livelong day, the livelong day,
And nibble at cheeses they are fed
Until they become cheesed off and away!

If, however, no atom decays,
The hammer holds fast
The flask is intact
No broken glass
No cyanide whiff
And to be sure, to be sure no feline stiff!

Then the tabby can lick its milk away
And play with the mouses the livelong day,
Alive as the lark in the clear air,
And so far as anyone here can see,
It's an existential, consummate
CCCCat-astrophe!

Mark. There's an equal probability
After one hour the cat will be
Either a pussycat-in-boots

With a grin and gay swashbuckling boots
Or in a dead state!
And that's the truth!

According to Schrodinger's wave theory
And Max Born's probabilities,
The box would hold our patient tabby
That's neither wholly alive or dead,
In a purgatorial custody,
A mixture of both possibilities.

Now a cat is a macroscopic lump,
A kilo of purring flesh and paws,
Made up of atoms and molecules.
Each one obeying quantum laws!
But the Wave Function of this story, we know,
Leaves the cat in a state that is rococo.

Hair and blood and gizzard and tail
And eye and backbone and ear and nail
With some extra bits for male, female,
Scattered and smeared across the wave
In a live-dead mix in the quantum state,
Grotesque, bizarre and out-of-the-way.

The Wave Function, a sea of possibilities,
A superposition of states,
Awaiting an agent to actualise
One singular, particular state.
This cat is a dead-and-alive farrago
Alloyed in a probabilistic limbo.

The cat in this state must be dead AND alive
Until we nervously look inside.
To create the physical pussycat
The Wave Function must be collapsed,
And Consciousness is the agent
That does the job and that is that!

This cat in this uncertain imbroglio
Allows mouses to nibble whatever all day,
In its unbelievable captivity
Until observation sets it free.
Still, the cat must know it is alive,
Dreaming milk and dreaming mice!

But until the moment it is seen
We wonder in what state it has been!
What? A cat observe himself perchance
To see its own Wave Function collapse?
Or a bacterium's sideways glance?
A case of to see or not to see?

For Bohr, to be or not to be,
Depends on what the observer sees.
The cat is neither dead NOR alive
So that can't be the floor of reality.
(Later Einstein put gunpowder in it
And blew the hapless cat to bits!)

Now in the Wave Function where we lay our scene
The cat is Alive and in Smithereens!
The probability interpretation

Of Schrodinger's wave equation
Is only resolved by observation—
The cat can have only one condition.

Open the box for the evidence.
Your Consciousness is the difference.
Reader don't giggle up your sleeve,
And that, as the man said, is that!
It seems you can't beat the Chinese!
Next time you eat a Chinese rat,
Remember that! Remember that!

Chapter Fifteen

The Glory of the Quantum, The E-P-R Paradox.

Albert Einstein (1879-1955) Boris Podolsky
(1896-1966) Nathan Rosen (1909-1995)

(Entanglement; Once atomic systems have been connected or Entangled,
they never separate. This remarkable property of non-locality demanded
action-at-a-distance or faster-than-light communication and implies
vast webs of interconnectivity between particles across the universe.)

UNIT ONE COULD ENTANGLEMENT BE REAL?

Einstein, Podolsky and Rosen (EPR) tried
To define what is real, what is incomplete.
Quantum Mechanics says information
Is transmitted instantaneously
Between two sister particles
No matter how far apart they might be.

Two systems entangled
Lose their Wave Functions
And merge into one Discarnate Whole,
A single waveform whose remotest parts
Are unmitigated and immediate,
An integrated Consciousness,

Each particle leaves a part
Of its being in the other's care,
So all particles in the universe
Are phase entangled; meaning, the Universe
Is in principle, one overall Wave Function,
An integrated Consciousness.

This Entanglement implies
Vast webs of connectivities
Between particles in the universe
In millions-of-miles-apart realities!
How do they communicate to one another?
Through an integrated Consciousness.

Are all things linked at the quantum scale?
Can Wave Functions have telepathy?
Take an unstable particle, stationary,
Decaying into two daughter ones,
That fly and spin in contrarious ways,
In that integrated Consciousness?

One must be "spin up",
The other "spin down",
Away, faraway, in both possible states.

Measure one. And then, and then,
The Wave Functions for both will collapse
In the integrated Consciousness.

The baby twins' eyes were all a fuzzball
Of green and red or any such hue
Until the midwife said "They're blue."
So was Entanglement true?
Einstein-Podolsky-Rosen said
"This is impossible. This is absurd.
No integrated Consciousness."

UNIT TWO NONSENSE!!! AN INTEGRATED-CONSCIOUSNESS?

"The time has come," the Walrus said*," to talk of many things,*
Of shoes—and ships—and sealing wax—and cabbages—and
kings—
And why the sea is boiling hot—and whether pigs have wings."
Lewis Carroll
"Denial is a river in Egypt."
Mark Twain

Einstein-Podolsky-Rosen said, I repeat,
"This is impossible.
This is absurd.
Quantum is inherently incomplete."

Is Quantum Mechanics' description true?
Some hidden irregularities we can't see?
Some hidden inequalities?
Know the twins' eyes were always blue.

Quantum mechanics is incomplete.
The Uncertainty Principle forbids
That simultaneous measurement of position
And momentum can ever find perfection.

Some say that such a quantum relation
Restricts a classical application.
But two particles can be in a state
In which they perfectly correlate.

Before measurement, both had existed
In a superposition of both possible states.
Measure one and the other's position can be
Established immediately with certainty,

Because of the perfect correlation.
But the second particle being far away
Was never affected physically
So, it must have knowledge and been Aware!!!

So All-There-Is in the Universe
Is All-Part-Of,
Is all-Blessed
In an Integrated Consciousness?

UNIT THREE LATENT CONSCIOUSNESS

*"The conscious mind is a house of awareness. The front door is our
face to the world. The backdoor is an entrance to other worlds.
Largely we are taught to disregard the back door."*
Jane Roberts

"The whole drift of my education goes to persuade me that the world
of our present conscious-world
is only one out of many worlds of consciousness that exist."
William James

Could this incredibly be true?
How could that particle be aware?
Does it have Latent Consciousness?
Is Quantum Mechanics incomplete?

In teleportation, you're sold a pup.
You can never obtain all information.
Thankfully with Scottie, I'll not sup
Should someone try to beam me up!

Can a particle with such possibilities
Ever be completely real?
Are there categorical imperatives?
Clear fundamental ontologies?

Weisskopf tried to put it straight—
"It enriches our view of nature's state."
Differences between the role of Theory
And the true Nature of Reality

Became a debate on philosophy.
So, could Entanglement be true?
A probabilities, no certainties game?
Or a complete Einsteinian paradigm?

UNIT FOUR DAVID BOHM (1917-1992)

"The Wave Function is a kind of mental aspect of an electron.
Maybe it is alive! What sense would it make to say it is not?"
David Bohm

After the Second World War, the United States
Foundered in anti-Communist paranoia.
David, this brilliant boy from Pennsylvania,
Was subpoenaed in 1948.

As a communist, he was arrested,
Even though nineteen of his close relatives
Died in Nazi concentration camps.
He knew atomic secrets. Was blacklisted.

He left for Sao Paulo in Brazil.
There his passport was confiscated
By American embassy officials.
But he knew more, as much as the mystic.

He saw the electron as a particle and a wave,
Jumping shells, nor passing in between,
Behaving like a total mystery.
Calculable, yes, but still the strangest philistine.

He dived into de Broglie's pilot wave theory,
Sunken to death in a Solvey grave,
Resurrected in the Schrodinger wave
And into Von Neumann's hidden variables,

Obscure secrets in the quantum mines,
Inaccessible to analysing metrics,
Not subject to the Uncertainty Principle
Whose predictions agree with Quantum Mechanics.

Variables that would lead to exact predictions,
Not just probabilities,
Between pairs of entangled electrons.
Things are or they are not.

Bohm found variables' mathematics
Fell foul of equations in quantum physics.
Proving quantum inconsistencies!
Improbabilities, improbabilities!

He liked the nominal "wavicle".
A real wave that guides the particle.
In the double slit experiment
The electron particle goes through one slit,

As the Wave Function splits, takes both routes,
And reunites when it slithers through.
Still, is such a wave a mathematical fiction?
Does it have a physical function too?

Reality is multi layered.
Our three-dimensional world he called
The Explicate Order.
It contains matter, space and time.

It permeates the Implicate Order,
An underlying, hidden, enfolded domain
We know as the Wave Function,
Beyond matter, space and time.

And a second enfolded Order
The Super-Information field of the universe
That organises and creates stable forms.
This he called the Super Implicate Order.

The universe is One, is Whole, with forms
Explicated, created, then enfolding
Back again in a ceaseless succession
Of enfolding and unfolding.

He presents a new relationship
Between the material and the mental,
Between matter and Consciousness.
This he calls Soma-Significance,

Two aspects of a single process.
Reader, the page you read is a Soma.
The Significance is the brain's process
Which the Mind understands.

So, the Soma has Significance
And what is Significance can be Soma.
It is the relationship between
Physical and mental, between body and soul.

The domain of the Wave Function
Is a vast ocean of mystical light

Which is One, Unbroken, Whole
With instantaneous connectedness.

As we shall see this superluminal connection
Actually exists where a "bit" of each being
Has a presence in the other's care,
And this "phase" connection,

This phase Entanglement remains
And connects them forever and forever.
This domain is only accessible to us
In altered states of Consciousness.

Things like yoga, meditation,
Mystical, meditative prayerfulness,
In the symbols of lucid dreaming,
And in "God is light, in Him there is no darkness."

UNIT FIVE JOHN STEWART BELL (1928-1990), THERE IS AN INVISIBLE REALITY

"Bell's work, which should apply to any fundamental theory of nature
(i.e. not just quantum theory),
could turn out to be one of the most important theoretical ideas of the
century."
J.P.McEvoy
"The most profound discovery of science."
Henry Stapp

An Irish physicist, John Stewart Bell,
Sharpened his teeth on the E-P-R paradox
And with a new theory cast a spell.

He developed the ingenious Inequality Principle
Based on correlated photons, (not electrons)
In which the polarization of light

Is detected instead of spin.
The principles are the same.
Will one photon affect the other?

He used ideas everyone could agree on
Except Einstein's condition of Locality,
(The speed of light.) Bell assumed this to be true.

But if experiments prove the Inequality was violated
This would mean his derivation was false.
Meaning nature is Non-Local.

Two particles that interact
And then move any distance apart
Will influence each other instantaneously.

He proved there are hidden variables
Deeper than we can understand,
Instantaneous interconnectednesses.

A high level of correlations
Between quantum particles outside our reality,
In an extra-dimensional space,

A Transcendental cyber place,
And that the quantum world exists
Independent of observation.

Einstein-Podolsky-Rosen's view was untenable
If Bell's Inequality Theorem, still a notion,
Could be proved by experimentation.

Clauser and Freedman put it to the test.
Some violations unfolded.
And then Alain Aspect buried it.

He found particles are entangled and measuring one
Affects the other Instantaneously,
Violating Einstein's edict on light speed.

Across this Non-Locality, faster than light's speed,
Nothing crosses the interval between
And influences act instantaneously.

They do not diminish with distance,
Without delay, without decay,
And are unmediated, unmitigated and immediate.

Ubiquitous connectivity,
One with the Absolute Consciousness,
Influences bred in a Timeless Domain.

Bell's mathematical Theorem proves
Our local reality is immersed
In the infinite realm of the Wave Function.

Yes, Einstein's view was no longer tenable
And anyway, by now he was gone. Albert goodnight!
Niels Bohr can now pose in the spotlight.

Where lies the quest for the quantum grail?
Where does the possible become the real?
And where awakens the Hidden Domain?

UNIT SIX HUGH EVERETT (1931-1982)
MANY WORLDS INTERPRETATION

"For Everett, the Wave Functions never collapse. Each and every
potential outcome
embodied in the Wave Function sees the light of day; the daylight
each sees, however, streams through its own separate universe."
Brian Greene

Hugh Everett, in truth, was not a nice man.
A chain-smoking, broken, dysfunctional,
Gambling physicist
But his horse is more than an also-ran!

In 1957, Everett's "Many Worlds interpretation"
Found every outcome of experimentation
Lives in the authentic reality,
In the Creator's ontology.

All quantum possibilities
Coexist in actual realities
In an array of Parallel Universes.
The impossible possibility?

He found the ghosts of Schrodinger's cat!
There's one where the cat is but a stiff!
In another he's wistfully eying the fish!
But to measure, observe, an impossible wish!

What if the Universe is split,
The whole Wave Function should collapse?
What if it doesn't? Mmm... What if?
Could every outcome possibly exist?

Like an amoeba reproduces
By dividing into two equal pieces
Which drift away with intelligent memories,
Two different paths in separate lives,

So his concept of the universe is enlarged
To include innumerable parallel universes,
So anything that quantum mechanics predicts
Could happen, does, in reality, happen!

In parallel worlds the possibility
Of time travel is a reality,
Expressed in accurate mathematics.
Go back in time to one universe.

Of the split, of course, you are unaware,
There is no contact between the pair.
You may go forward to another
Existing in two relative states,

Superimposed, one on another,
Unable, unwilling to contact the other,
One with a dead cat,
A live one the other!

Go back in time and stick your Gran,
To undo a given inheritance plan!
Go into the future and poison your father
To certify he won't die hereafter!

Hold it! This is beautiful anarchy.
But slightly imperfect copies of me
Constantly splitting would have to be,
I pray, irreconcilable with the real me.

Copies are mere speculation.
Space it seems is more dense.
A story very hard to align
With orthodox, common sense.

Chapter Sixteen

The Wonder that is the Future.

UNIT ONE THE SPICE OF LIFE.

> *"My soul needs to be honoured with a new dress woven*
> *From green and blue things and arguments that cannot be proven."*
> Patrick Kavanagh

In the past, the powerful dogs of uncertainty
Slept under history's towering authority;
Churches and States, stomping for centuries.

But doubt need not be feared but extolled.
O welcome the dark, dark night of the soul!
Religion and Science must walk hand-in-hand.

The mystical concept of God still stands,
And ignorance, doubt are a part of it.
It's fine. There is no knowing it.

Science and experiments disprove superstition,
Fake miracles and blind reincarnation.
Knowledge defines life's evolution,

The ethics, aesthetics and metaphysics,
The beauty and thought all still remain.
The poet can indict a lyric's refrain,

The painter emblazon in purple and blue,
The singer the sweetest notes can intone,
The sculptor can chisel out bronze or stone,

The priest can ignite the flames of the soul,
The Truth be inscribed in symbol and scroll.
Stand by the sea's plash a moonlit night,

Look at the stars' tremblent, twinkling light;
Feel the mystical weight of mystery fall
Out of infinity on you, so small.

The freedom from certainty brings insight,
Allows us adjudicate wrong from right,
And probability comes into play.

Sometimes coincidence has its day.
A prayer can kill a cancer cell
Just as medicine can make you well,

And blue and green aliens can never be
As real as the particles we can't see.
Each one of the disciplines we were taught

Are shades of the same ineffable Truth.
Medicine, ethics, epistemology,
Logic, physics, faith, cosmology,

Scholasticism, poetry, psychology,
Pantheism, chemistry, philosophy,
Bibliolatry, fiddlesticks and codology.

And Life is a physic defined, refined,
Redefined, derefined, refined and defined.
Those with some Mystical inspiration

Who reveal to us, simples, some revelation,
Are ones who often defy convention---
Geniuses-- who reach the secret station.

UNIT TWO ALWAYS DOUBT THE TRUTH

*"It is always the best policy to speak the truth, unless of course
you are an exceptionally good liar."*
Jerome K. Jerome
*"The hero of my tale—whom I love with all the power of my soul,
whom I have tried to portray
in all his beauty, who has been, is and will be beautiful—is Truth."*
Leo Tolstoy

Truth is part of the essence we are
And while certainty is never far,
We await the Truth and while we wait
Doubt is an essential wing of faith.

Paradigms change in history.
Theories can be contradictory.
All Truth lies in the simplicity,
In the limits of our own reality.

The moonlight's authenticity,
The orchid's pale integrity,
The joy of knowing beauty,
Receiving and giving charity,

The virtues of faith and hope and love
Are the essence of the mystery.
The Quantum Theory stands sublime,
And it makes the real and unreal rhyme.

Nothing created has happened by chance.
Can we know the Dancer from the dance?
Fiddlestrings twang their music so sweet.
Can we separate the melody from the sheet?

The waters that crash on the moonlit sand;
Are you a whoosh or a Mystical Glance
Of part of Infinity within our grasp,
A bloom of Consciousness?

Are six-cornered snowflakes, unique, so fine,
But shades of the Omniscient Divine?
Such fundamentals stamped so fine
With fingerprints, hallmarks of the Divine.

Even seemingly empty space is full
Of a seething sea of virtuals
Which appear in infinitesimal epochs of time,
A turbulent pool of energy
That strips and rips the heart
Of the Spacetime fabric apart!

Is it all a camino taken step upon step,
An inevitable sequence of cause and effect
That grew from an Absolute Consciousness,
A Knowing, Ineffable Creator's act?

UNIT THREE WHAT'S TWO AND TWO?

"There is a wonder in and of our shrunken mortality and our
scrabbling appetites
which maybe prayer or maybe drama or maybe a song or a dance
or a breeze in the air can sometimes fleetingly catch hold of."

Two and two add up to four
But we must perpetually
Be open to the possibility
They may well be less, they may well be more.
In different realities there may be
To us unknown possibilities.
Two and two might well be three
Or God almighty! Snakes alive!
Two and two might well be five.

The Artist in the kingdom of Four
Compared to his masterpiece is more.

The creative Consciousness
That softly opens wide the door
To rooms that hold Creation's store
Must have access to other floors,
Mansions of wonder, rooms galore,
Of realities that we can't explore.
Authenticity as yet unknown.

Those different realities may be alive,
Worlds where we could not survive
Without His touch, His benign smile,
The Marvellous we dream about,
The dreams we marvel at in sleep,
The wonders of incredulity,
The wonders of possibilities,
The wonders of why and what might be,
Of all He created and oversees.

For me there is only One universe
With habitats for indefinities,
For finities, for infinities,
For unimaginable galaxies,
Unimaginable velocities,
Unimaginable energies,
Unimaginable complexities,
Unimaginable simplicities,
Unimaginable diversities.

They all interact and intersperse,
Interpenetrate and express
The wonder of the world we are in,

Following a singular set of rules
That unfolds from a Hidden Consciousness
Into one Continuous Dimension.
So know,
Science fiction gimmicks are crap
And alien, mythical tales obscure.

The monuments of man that survive, overlap,
Are testament to our antecedents
Who were gifted faith and kept it,
Faith so precious to the heart,
Who knew the Truth,
Nothing but the Truth
Of Conscious Verisimilitude.
So we wonder why we wonder why
We wonder why we wonder…

Why we marvel lazily under
This lapis lazuli blue sky;
Why we hitch-hike around forty shades
Of viridescent green;
Why we stumble in dog days, parched,
Across shimmering sand;
Why we skate along the ice and snow
While the chill winds blow

And touch, taste, hear, feel and see
Multiple colours in between.
We wonder why we wonder why
We wonder why we wonder...

UNIT FOUR THE BEAUTY OF THE UNIVERSE.

*"The Good, the True, the Beautiful! Alas, the Good is so often untrue,
the True so often unbeautiful, the Beautiful so often not good."*
Isaac Goldberg

All was fast forward, no reverse,
In an expanding jewel-box universe
Of jewels and pearls with millions of hues,
Lemons, oranges, yellows and blues,

Indigos, violet's, reds and greens,
Azure greys and aqua marines,
Cinnamons, reds, galactic pinks,
Apricots, sapphires and citrines,

Moon creams, interstellar winks and blinks,
Ebonies, turquoises, damascenes,
Lavenders, blacks and malachite greens,
Incarnadine stains, phosphorescences,

Chocolates, chestnuts and magnolias,
Purples, vermillion and gardenias,
Cherries, oranges, carnation reds,
Magentas, carmines and dingy lead.

The colours of garden flowers round here
Were born in the chaotic atmosphere
Of supernovae – exploding stars-
Billions of light years stretching afar,

With radio waves that filled all space,
Intensity intense in every place.
And antigravity's dominance grew
Wherever it is, if only we knew!

Beauty translucent, beauty opaque,
The music of the spheres was played
And replayed over and over again.
Notes cacophonous and euphonious,

Jazz-time, jive and boogie woogie,
Bass, soprano, coloratura,
Nocturne, fugue diminuendo,
Symphony and psalm accelerando.

Music it was and the Powers-that-be
Gave it the perfect balance to be.
But out in the cantons of the unknown
There could be more substances than we know?

There is no such thing as empty space.
Limitless possibilities interface.
Interacting particles create, annihilate.
Appearing from nothing, back to nothing fade.

A Conscious, vibrant, living place.
A seething maelstrom of subatomic space.
Empty space is a seething mess
Of restless, ceaseless turbulence

And unpredictable randomness,
Unless we embody a symmetry
For all that Consciousness
In mathematical equations.

Still complex phenomena remain
Like the inner workings of your brain,
With its illimitable Consciousness
Outside the mathematical domain.

Such incomprehensibility
To which utter simplicity gave birth
Growing to such complexity
To where we are on Planet Earth.

Speculations of the Multiverse
Allow oodles of possibilities,
With all their random uncertainties,
And indefinite unpredictabilities.

Effects that lead to a future spoken
In the language of probabilities.
The hidden critical complexities
Are mere shadows of the mysteries,

And this storm-tossed voyage still unfolds
Recesses hidden deep down Nature's hold
And Heaven's Absolute Consciousness,
Call it God or Heaven or What-You-Will,

Filled with the all-knowing Presences
From which springs all existences
Whose energy is Whole, is One,
Is a Consciousness Continuum,

A spectrum of Infinite Consciousness
While each thing longs after its own truth,
Aware of what it longs to be, to become,
Through its own innate, imbued creativity

In this universe's sweet reality
That leaves us wondering, wondering...
O We wonder why we wonder why
We wonder why we wonder...

UNIT FIVE HERE WE ARE ON PLANET EARTH.

"Earth is here so fine that, just tickle her with a hoe, and she laughs with a harvest." Douglas Jerrold

Here we are on Planet Earth,
Ordinary place in the suburbs.

We have pulled some strings
On the nature of things
But know little of what future millennia will bring,
Or the teasing mysteries that wonder brings,
Or where the Mystical begins,
Or where the Ineffable spirit sings,
Or beyond the physics, what physics brings.
But we know the joy curiosity brings.

Here we are on Planet Earth,
Where humanity bows in a humble place.

The holiest altar in all space,
Peering down the infinitesimal place,
Down the scrambled, complex recesses,
Undreamed-of primordial addresses,
Larger and smaller than we can chase.
Where most of it is, is anyone's guess,
Where Dark Matter and Dark Energy race,
Wonders yet to be addressed.

Here we are on Planet Earth,
A rendezvous more complex than we can know.

Since thirteen point seven billion years ago,
Myriads of fine-tuned mysteries grow.
Why oh why does it bother to be?
How did laws of nature come to be?
Who or what could have dreamed this show?
An impartial, infallible Impresario!
Still, uncertainties, possibilities flow.
The more we understand the less we know!

Here we are on Planet Earth,
Searching the ghostly signposts.

Along infinite motorways we go,
Watching for miracles to unfold,
In the half light, in darkness, in shadow,
Through a thin veil fretted in blues and greens

Longing for the mystical, the unseen,
Where flowers are singing in colours never seen,
And all our dreams and hopes are blessed
In the One Iridescent Consciousness.

And as we wait we are wondering,
Wondering why we wonder why
We wonder why we wonder...

UNIT SIX THE SEARCHERS

*"Knock and the door will open, seek and you will find, ask and you
will be given..."* Matt. 7,7-8
"The heaven of each is but what each desires."
Thomas Moore

Some seek the Transcendent in a Prayer,
In the beauty of Art, in loving Care,

Or in all the infinite varieties there,
While others traverse deepest levels of Truth,

Bruising the body to pleasure the soul,
Communing the joy the unknown brings,

Discerning, seeking, searching to embrace
Symbols that lead to the ultimate place.

Mathematicians seek out number and score,
Physicists existence, time and space,
Scientists observe and seek out the facts
To verify empirical hypotheses

Biologists desire what secrets there be
In Life's astonishing variety,

Artists illume the darkness within,
While poets set darknesses echoing.

All parts of a single Reality,
A single, unbroken Consciousness.

All Nature is woven in Communion
And all its aspects intersperse
In our micro-macro-universe.

Particles, forces, adjustable Constants,
All vague reflections of our ignorance.

Chapter Seventeen

Keep on the Sunny Side

UNIT ONE THE ANTHROPIC PRINCIPLE

"The brain is a three-pound mass you can hold in your hand that can
conceive
of a universe a hundred-billion light-years across."
Marian Diamond

Brandon Carter in nineteen seventy-three,
The five hundredth anniversary
Of Nicholas Copernicus who proved that we
Have no privileged place in the Universe,

Claimed we are inevitably
Privileged by the sheer improbability
Of a universe tuned for us to exist.
The Paradox of the Anthropic Principle.

The Universe in a highly structured state,
Designed for life, for ancestors that stretch
Along a highly improbable chain of events.
Break one link and you're not here!

The Universe that knew we were coming!
It provided essential requisites.
Laws and coincidences conspire
To within fractions of one percentile

To make the Earth propitious for Life,
For carbon-based intelligence.
Like winning the national lottery,
Week in, week out, perpetually!

Or a monstrous sequence of accidents
Defined by mathematical physicists?
Or a deep-based Designer Universe
Set in majestic Transcendence?

The latter from all the evidence.
The presence of intelligent life
Is part explanation that what is, is, and points down
The one creative lane we were born.

Our Conscious Awareness will never shirk
From the clear fact that no evidence can prove
Our existence is a meaningless quirk,
Rather a transcendental Act of Love.

If Earth were five million miles closer at hand,
The Sunlight's intensity would create a dark room,
A dry, barren, desert wasteland.
Our snowdrops would never bloom.

If Earth were one million miles farther away,
The Sunlight's tenuity would make it up to its ears
A frozen, tenantless castaway,
With a gloomy, darkling atmosphere.

If planet Earth' magnetic field
Did not shield us far and near,
Then invasive bursts of radiation
Would come sleeting through the biosphere.

If the fundamental Constants of physics
Were not so finely tuned
The probability of life would be so low,
Our chances to exist would be in ruins.

In the critical density of matter,
Remember an imbalance of decimal
One hundred and eighteen zeros with one,
Would certify life was never on!

If the strong nuclear force, that binds
The protons and neutrons in place,
Were to be the slightest stronger,
No stars, no life, no human race.

If electromagnetic and gravity forces
Did not have their precise balance,
Their equilibrium would never hold,
No supernovae, planets and elements.

If cosmic background radiation variations
Due to uncertain quantum vibrations
Differed by one in a hundred thousand,
Stars would crash towards desolation,

Or else would slow, would slow.
In each case, a me and a you would be a no, no, no.
If the ratio between the masses
Of the proton and the neutron

Had a teeny, weeny difference,
All the stars would burn out
And atoms have no existence.
Are you thinking all these were accidents?

Whether it's a weak anthropic principle, (WAP)
Or a strong anthropic principle, (SAP)
Or a participatory anthropic principle, (PAP)
Or a final anthropic principle, (FAP)

There are certain Constants in physics
That are conducive to giving us Life,
Principles that allow us to survive.
No Completely Ridiculous Anthropic Principle!!!

No matter! For existence to take root,
When you eliminate the impossible,
What remains, however improbable,
Must be closer to the Truth!

Such illimitable precision.
Hardly things that happened by chance!
Otherwise all would accelerate too fast
To give time for matter to coalesce,

Or go too slow, no Big Bang in reverse.
No. Micro and macro intertwined-just-
Where stars are born, supernovae burst,
Vacuum energy balance a must,

Creating particles, elements, forces.
You can say, for sure, we are stardust.
A contrived illusion or Designer stuff?
Us

So staggeringly small, impeccably precise,
So startlingly immaculate.
Sing!
Oh! Sing with joyous voice!

Nothing we know is so finely tuned
In all the physics of the Universe.

UNIT TWO MAN, THE OBSERVER AND CREATOR

"You enter the brain through the eye, march up the optic nerve, round and round the cortex looking behind each neuron, and then, before you know it, you emerge into daylight on the spike of a motor nerve impulse, scratching your head and wondering where the self is."
Daniel Dennett

"Ex umbris et imaginibus in veritatem."
J.H. Newman

"A self-made man? Yes—and he worships his Creator."
William Cowper

The idea that the observer
Creates everyday reality
Means that Consciousness
Is the one ingredient necessary
In making/remaking the universe

And alters the old school view
Because the physicist and the mouse too
Are part of that same universe
Which is always, in a sense,
There observing itself.

This implies there's a hierarchy
Of Consciousnesses,
Each state with potentialities
Of actual occurrences.
But one probability

Is brought into actual reality
By the observer's view

So
He becomes the creator,
The mind of the observer.

His Consciousness,
Gives form to the potential
Which then exhibits
Properties that are material,
Particles that are alive.

They resonate with the Mind,
Energy Resonances,
Electromagnetic, gravitational,
Responding to each other,
Integrating with the observer creating reality.

And above or below our universe
May be hidden universes invisible and unknown,
Part of the Absolute Consciousness,
Unknowable manifestations
In the domain of the Wave Function.

Chapter Eighteen

The Mysteries Of Creation

"When we try to complete as far as possible the quantum theoretic account of the electron gun, we include first the scintillation screen, and then the photographic film, and then the developing chemicals, and then the eye of the experimenter... and then her brain. For the brain is made of atoms, electrons and nuclei, and so why should we hesitate to apply Wave Mechanics... at least if we were smart enough to do the calculations for such a complicated assembly of atoms? For beyond the brain is ... the Mind. Surely the Mind is not material? Surely here at last we come to something which is distinctly different from the glass screen and the gelatine film and..."
JOHN STUART BELL

MYSTERY NUMBER ONE THE MEANING OF EXISTENCE

"We are such stuff as dreams are made on, And our little life is rounded with a sleep."
William Shakespeare

Existence is the simplest mystery.
We perceive that we exist. Ask why?
Each question followed by a thousand "whys".
More an infinite shuffling, say, with a sigh.
A question listening to itself
Where all the answers are intensely blessed.

Man is thrown into existence,
A mariner tossing on dangerous seas,
Under a quizzical, twinkling heaven,
In the spell of ever-devouring time
Seeking the meaning in the design,
The grace notes, the miraculous.

We are all butterflies, mayflies,
Briefly, tenuously flickering,
On a strangely, beautiful place.
We linger on the cosmic shores,
Wanderers, we open doors into the dark,
With an eye out for shimmers of light.

What is the meaning of Being?
The question history has posed,
In faith, in hope and in love exposed,
The sense of meaning for a life
That cherishes the future with shortening breath,
Knowing the only certainty is death.

175

The self and others and time and space
Locked in an indissoluble embrace,
With reverence for the inexplicable,
Of what is dearest, nearest us.
Ineffable faith holds the mystery,
The Untouchable, invisible to us.

That moment one becomes alive
Makes one eligible for death.
But living, O that is something else
And therefore, is no threat!
Physical death is the individual, the passionate,
The existential, universal fate.

And time is irreversible,
The past always comes late.
Thoughts of immortality
Spring from a space-enduring faith.
The throbbing heart of time is Now!
The blinding infinitely intense Wow!

The wonder, fear, decision, oh act! desire,
The mystique of the Now alive!
Each moment a twinkling of awakening,
Of awareness, present in the mind,
When the real intersects with the numinous
Each instant in the trajectory of time,

Where we welcome sunlight with open arms
Or seek a cover from the storm.
It flames and flickers in the light,

Free, desirable, spontaneous,
Touched by the Transcendent Absolute,
Cardinal, mundane, miraculous.

Always in the midst of life
It lies about us everywhere.
We view it inside, where it hides,
In the light of Consciousness, of Being-There.
This the pure and absolute boundary,
The beginning, the end of all we are,

Revealing itself in faith, in hope,
In love that reveals itself to love.
And the actual, factual realities,
The select ideologies of discovery,
Raises science on its sacred plinth,
Among transcendental treasuries.

We must look in the eyes of the mystery,
Abandon the watchers in caves of shadows,
Walk into the light of truth.
And if we are blinded by the light,
Allow all we see there illuminate,
So we grow to a greening branch and root.

And though we know there will ever be
It's simple impenetrability,
We search the inexhaustible mysteries
Of our environs wherever that be.
And the ineffable residue that we find
Informs the soul and delights the mind.

So we seek to know our deepest selves
In the midst of where we dare.
Existence is being Self-Aware,
Of our being, of our restlessness,
Seeking the self that seeks His love
While He reveals Himself to faith,
Keeping us all in His loving care

MYSTERY NUMBER TWO THE SIZE OF THE UNIVERSE

"To see a World in a Grain of Sand
And a Heaven in a Wild Flower,
Hold Infinity in the palm of your hand
And Eternity in an hour."
William Blake

In one ten thousandth of a sec
All was crammed in the quantum speck.
Inflation put its foot on the gas
And off the winds of existence flew,
Zillions of lightning bolts out of the blue.
And all the imprinted irregularities
Were just the right size from which we grew.
We lay like snowdrops in the driven snow

Out in the suburbs of cosmic space,
A very, very, dangerous place,
And it dropped us here in a fluctuation
Of thermal equilibrium.
Time has followed the pilgrim's progress

And the laws of physics in time-reverse,
Tell us the age of the Universe.
And the insignificance of our star, the Sun.

Among thousands of billions, it is but one,
Sitting in a whorl of the Milky Way,
One of billions of galaxies stretching away,
Travelling ten thousand miles a sec.
The nearest galaxy, Andromeda,
Is three million light-years away
So light from it set out before the birth
Of the earliest humans roaming the Earth!

The nearest star, Proxima Centuri,
Is four point two light-years away!
The nearest cluster of galaxies, Virgo,
Made of a thousand galaxies
Is fifty million light-years from here!
The farthest galaxy cluster, vaguely clear
Is ten billion light-years from here!
Hubble and Humason have been there.

So, we see galaxies that we know
As they were millions, billions of years ago!
So where are they now? No. Let that one go!
Methinks it better to let that one go!
The light travelling all that time
Draws a limit on the horizon line.
The most distant flashes we see now
Are the lights that set out those years ago.

They have since, headlong, been travelling,
While all of space has been expanding.
The whole caboodle speeding up!
Those objects that we think we see
Are forty billion light years from here,
And as we speak, they may, may not be.
Out in the suburbs of godknowswhere,
In regions of possibilities,

The unseeable and unforeseeable
Shadows move towards eternity.
Unknowable realms we will never see.
Nearer to home the electrical attraction
Compared to gravity attraction
Between proton and electron
Is ten thousand trillion, trillion, trillion
Times larger, that's unfathomable!

Like the size of the universe to an electron
Or the mass of the universe to a proton
And the electromagnetic force
Is one hundred billion times stronger
Than the weak nuclear force which is
Ten million, billion, billion, billion
Times stronger than weakest gravity!
An infinitessimal part of eternity!

It is grotesque, unbelievable and bizarre
That there could be billions, billions of stars
Whirling along on their merry way
In a single galaxy, the Milky Way.

Gigantic colossals that crunch and burn,
Tens of thousands the size of the Sun,
At massive speeds they crash and churn
In a galactic dance of perpetual fun.

It is grotesque, unbelievable and bizarre,
That our galaxy of billions, billions of stars
Is one of billions of galaxies,
Near infinite oodles of energies,
Musters of clusters and synergies,
That crunch and crumble, slash and bend,
Create, uncreate and recreate
In places where imagination ends.

And to think that all of this consists
Of but four per cent of all that exists
Puts in perspective the stuff we missed
In our child-like view of the Universe.
The rest is Dark Matter, Dark Energy,
Stuff we can neither hear nor see
Because it will nor interact
With our visible reality.

Forgive me God, invisible, visible,
And pardon me if I'm sentimental,
But it lies beyond my comprehension
To imagine all this as accidental.
What kind of awesome Inventor could
Make billions, billions of galaxies,
Each one with billions, billions of stars,
Spring from a singularity?

Create our galaxy, the Milky Way,
With billions in orbits, billions astray,
Blue stars in birth-pangs, in nebulae,
Scattering, cooking in supernovae,
Ordered turbulence, silent blare,
While those billions of galaxies reciprocate
The same procedures in all of space
Stretching faintly far away?

Know that Heisenberg's Principle states
That energy, momentum are partners in space.
Particle eruptions, annihilations,
Wild electromagnetic field oscillations,
Weak and strong force fluctuations,
Tell us any empty region of space
Is a teeming, chaotic, frenzied place
On cosmic, microscopic scales.

Twisting, frothing, turbulent foam,
With a quantum unfamiliar face.
These quantum fluctuations are not in line
With a smooth model of time and space,
A feature of General Relativity,
Its smooth and gently curving geometry
Breaks down at the quantum Planck length,
A millionth, billionth, billionth, billionth centimetre.

That makes the two terrific Theories,
Quantum and Relativity
Incompatible.
Two contradictory tabernacles.

Perhaps Superstring Theory will find a way
To resolve and unify them one day,
Or a unified M-theory may some day
Encompass all in one tapestry.

And to think that all this space was needed
To set the seeds of our existence
And all this time was needed too
To sprout the shoots of our intelligence,
This foil for our insignificance,
Or is it our magnificence?
The stupendous size of the universe.
Another cosmological coincidence?

UNIT THREE TOUCHING BASE WITH INFINITY IN THE INFINITY HOTEL

"That is infinite, this is infinite, from infinite arises infinite, when
infinite is subtracted
from infinite, what is left is infinite."
Sanscrit
"There are only two things we know that are infinite. The universe
and human stupidity.
But I'm not sure about the first."
Albert Einstein

How do we touch base with infinity?
In the transcendental creed of faith?
Or watching sunsets in yellow and gold,
Marvelling at the wonders of old?
Or in the beauty we can behold
In a prayer, a poem or the dawn's red light?

Or the indifferent, mystical sky at night
Startled by sprinkled, star-spangled light?

Contemplating the infinite plays
A salient Significance in our lives.
We see our endings in beginnings,
Our sharings in accomplishings,
The potentialities we fear,
The possibilities we hold dear,
Unravelling our creative life,
Our role in Nature's way,
And in this tremendous universe,
Pondering the Infinite Love
In the Eternal Consciousness.

Can anyone tell where infinity ends?
In the final printout another page pends.
Are indefinities, enigmas, paradoxes true?
What is infinity to you?

THE INFINITY HOTEL, A FABLE

There once was an Infinity Hotel
Where every single room was full.
One day a weary guest arrived.
No room!
The manager, Hilbert, found a solution.

Put the new guest in room number one.
Move room one guest to room two.
Room two guest to room three,
Etcetera, etceterae, eternally.

Full occupancy!
To the end of infinity, with no exclusion!

NEXT DAY...
An infinite number of guests all the way
From a neighbouring galaxy wished to stay,
The ultimate reunion with spaceships full
Of incidental, encircling aliens.
The manager, Hilbert, found a solution.

Let each guest multiply their room by two.
So one goes to two, two to four, three, four and nine
To six, eight and eighteen on down along the line.
All the even rooms are full!
All the odd rooms await a guest!
Both to the end of infinity, with no exclusion!

Any and all new arrivals now
Can, in beds of down, be cooped,
Can luxuriate, be warm as toast,
In all the odd numbered rooms.
Full occupancy!
Room service is no easy matter
But no one is out in the cold.

THE MORNING AFTER ...
However, the guests in the even rooms,
After all the towing, all the lugging,
Wrenching, dragging and cruciation,
Queuing, lifts and humiliation,
Next day, disgruntled, all go away.
Hardly good business, you may say!

That's fifty per cent occupancy? It stinks!
Closure! Recession! The manager thinks.
The manager, Hilbert, found a solution.

Mmm... Leave the guests in room one and three,
Room two a store for portmanteaus, brief cases.
Move all the odd guests along the line,
Three, five, seven, nine, eleven, thirteen,
To rooms four, five, six, seven, eight and nine,
And on and on to full occupancy!
Notice, reader, no new guest came! Fine!
To the end of infinity, with no exclusion!

NEXT DAY...
An infinite number of sister hotels
From an infinite number of galaxies
Are going too, through their cosmic recessions,
And restructuring accommodations.
Emails! Closures! Ultimate strategies!

An infinite number of hotel managers,
Cleaners, waitresses, cooks, ushers
And receptionists get their walking papers.
Sacked and made redundant. Still,
They save an infinite salary bill.

It stinks! The manager, Hilbert, thinks.
"All the guests from our sister hotels
Must be moved to a cell,"
Says the CEO, "at the Infinity Hotel!"
"This Hotel is full!" Hilbert declares.

"Find more rooms!"
The CEO blares. Then he glares. Then he stares.
Methinks an infinite problem looms!

THAT EVENING...
Infinite spaceships blacken the skies.
The manager ponders. A receptionist cries.
The chamber maids take to swatting the flies.
And sad, sad to say, the chief telephonist dies.

An usher suggests the use of primes?
All primes are divisible only by themselves and one.
And they are unique and number infinity.
The manager thinks. This could be fun!
Hotel 1 gets rooms 2, 4, 8, 16, 32...
Hotel 2 gets rooms 3, 9, 27, 81...
Hotel 3 gets rooms 5, 25, 625...
Hotel 4 gets rooms 7, 47, 343...
And on and on so everyone has a room.
Al the rooms will have, if I'm right,
Different occupants at all given times!
Still all the rooms that are not powers of primes
Will be conspicuously tenantless.

The Manager, Hilbert, is stricken with grief.
His job will be on the line.
He may have accommodated an infinite infinites
But there's a maze of unoccupied rooms,
An infinity of idle rooms!

He reads the works of Leonard Euler;
Exponential functions,
Imaginary numbers,
Trigonometrical functions
And analyses infinitorums
But how can you dovetail and shuffle
Guests from numberless residences
Into one interminable cuffuffle?

NEXT MORNING…
To solve this loophole (for an infinite fee)
He telephones Management Consultancy Agency.
They criss and they cross and they intersperse
Their linsey-woolsey inquisitiveness
And finally draw up a table
Of the arriving guest's old room number
And the old hotel number from where they came.

Guest (1,1) to room 1, (1,2) to 2, (2,2) to 3, (2,1) to 4,
Guest (1,3) to 5, (2,3) to 6, (3,3) to 7, (3,2) to 8, (3,1) to 9,
Guest (1,4) to 10, (2,4), (3,4), (4,4), (4,3), (4,3), (4,2), (4,1)
And on and on and on and on
So all the guests got a room of their own
And no room is left unoccupied!

The Manager was apopleptic with joy!
The countless receptionists he began to employ
Accommodate all the guests anew
As rooms become available and so all
Are stitched into the mingled yarn. Phew!

It has taken time but what an achievement;
Occupancy back to one hundred per cent!

Room service buzzes. Revenue flows.
Restaurants dish out sumptuous dishes
At jammed, swingeing, entertainment shows
To incalculable, grubbing voluptuaries.

WEEKS LATER...
But after a while cracks began to abound,
Ushers sought counselling for suicide.
Waitresses took orders as they cried.
Barmen got high on formaldehyde.
Receptionists fainted.
The manager smiled at his small oversight!
Content there was no empty room to be found!

Profits and costs are prodigious until
An infinite tax liability bill
Drops softly down across the manager's desk.
How in god's name can he counteract this?
Pay it. We can do without overkill!
Infinite profits will be infinite still.

The accountant has kept the tax rate low
But when applied to an infinite number of bills
The result is infinite still!
But there are limitless complexities
In managing exhaustless guests
From thundering numbers of galaxies
In a stupendous cosmos without end
Amen.

SOME DAYS LATER...

The manager overnight becomes deranged.
The receptionists go off to Spain.
Some things need to be rearranged.
Sorry, infinitely radical change is required.
Then the Board of Management resigned.
There is nothing left but to close up shop.

THE END RESULT...

Ridiculous? Some things never change!
They close up shop and the truth to tell
Create a Minimalist Hotel.
No guests, no rooms, no profits, no costs.
The Ultimate Hotel-Absolute- Zero.

Absolute silence powers through the booms.
The atoms of ghosts throng the rooms.
Phantom memories still the walls
Of stairs that go down to empty halls.
There is nobody here at all, at all.

A doll is poised at the grand piano
Soundlessly eternally about to play.
No brandies, no mixers in the bars.
What once had meaning has gone too far.

All the lights are out. The atoms sleep.
Quiescent electrons freeze, seek peace.
Only the darkness illuminates.
Only the heart of silence breathes.
THE END.

MYSTERY NUMBER FOUR THE LAWS OF NATURE

> *"Number is the measure of all things."*
> Pythagoras
> *"The book of Nature is written in mathematics."*
> Gallileo

The architecture of the Universe
Is built on the symmetrical,
Invisible, mathematical rules
And on concepts theoretical.

A new law leads to novel contexts
And hence to new phenomena.
But all the theories of cosmic surmise
Will end if one morning the Sun will not rise.

And though Sunrise sang this morning's refrain
There is no guarantee it will sing again.
That it will is a humble act of faith
In Mother Nature's regular dates.

Absolute laws are eternal,
Embodied in maths equations,
And omniscient, for they inform
And command the right instructions.

While scientists make discoveries
As though they were their inventions,
They are but simple figments
Of finite imaginations.

Laws exist in the things we see.
In our daily kitchen reality.
Something there is about a wall.
It's always there, in spring, in fall.

But we cannot see the atoms at all,
Shadowy listeners on stairways
That go down to a cryptic hall.
Did you ever smell a quantum wave?

Sense its quivering invisibility?
And all those feelings, informations,
Memories, visible sensations,
Mental manifestations

Of beauty, thought and calculations,
The poetic virtuousity of a ballerina's elegance,
The wonder of an inspiration,
The arrogance of insolence,

The indifference of a vacant lot,
The formulae of scenic paths,
The insolence of arrogance,
Often written in beautiful maths?

Over time, some indispensable laws
Have been dispensed with, put away.
Is Earth the centre of the Universe?
Do lines follow Euclid's geometry?

The answer was "yes" but now we know
The answer is a definite "no"!
Mathematics' laws only go so far.
And they get stuck! Still, the door is ajar.

A deeper symmetry reveals
Holistic, mystical ethereals.
Mathematics, mathematics,
An abstract landscape that exists.

A jungle explored by physicists,
Revealing secrets already there,
Truths ethereal, miraculous,
Through man's astonishing mindscape.

Sometimes Consciousness bursts out.
Sudden revelations, dramatic euphoria,
Burrowing deep down Nature's code
To uncover universal laws in a blink,

Fathom the cryptic clues and link
Solutions in a coherent Whole,
Grasping the abstract from Nature's soul
In one brief mathematical stroke.

Who designed these laws of nature?
Who assigned the ratio of number?

Look at how we measure the spectrum.
Radio waves are metres, kilometres.
Micro waves are in centimetres.
Infrared hundreds of millimetres.

Visible light hundreds of micrometres.
Ultra violet, one hundred million to a metre.
X rays, ten million to a centimetre.
Gamma rays infinitesimal nanometres.

And the mass of a particle and its wavelength
Have a precise relationship.
The mass by velocity always is
Planck's Constant, a decimal point

With twenty-six zeros, six, six, two, six.
So small, so small. Hardly there at all.
A stitch in the heavens' embroidered cloth!
But it is. It is. And the balance sticks.

When the particle goes twice as fast
Its wavelength is halved. See the trick!
Applying to anything, everything.
So Who assigned these numbers?

Who gave the electron its energy bubble
As it flips around the nuclear shell?
The proton two thousand times it's mass.
The neutron similar more or less.

The nucleus a millionth billionth of the space.
So matter is mostly emptiness!
Who can say where an electron might be
In its speeding, stable resonance?

Pairs of electrons, share, combine,
In chains with bits and bobs attached
Much like children holding hands.
Atoms with atoms form molecules,

In the beautiful chemistry of life.
Paul Dirac, extraordinary ratios found
Down in the quantum underground.
Ten to the power of forty, of eighty.

Light speed, the age of the Universe,
Electrons, neutrons, protons, must be
The consequences of a hidden reality,
One that as now we cannot see.

They seem like strange coincidences
Of deeper, elusive relationships,
Inexplicable evidences
That physicists had somehow missed.

Mysterious strangers that characterise
The Universe's structure, its physics laws.
Paul had no faith but had limitless faith
In the special possibilities Creation gave.

There are some strange characteristics
Evident in the mathematics
Of a Creator's intelligent physics,
A key to unlock the creative cosmics.

The universe follows perfect rules.
We cannot know initial conditions.
A tiny error widens its ripples
Like a pebble plopped in a pond that is still.

Life's Geometer, Being itself,
Breathed fire into earth and water,
Creator and Cause of a Universe
That exists because it aughter.

It provides creative potentialities
Which Mother Nature actualises
Through evolutionary properties
Into creeping, richest varieties.

From random fluctuations
Come order, regularity,
Bland and beautiful complex things.
One man's irrationality is another's creativity.

Beyond quantum unpredictability,
Beyond quantum mechanics there must be
Bundles of laws beyond our sagacity,
Buried in invisibility.

Different dimensions, strange and rare,
New interpretations, mysteries there,
Deep down burrows disturb if you dare,
Down the ineffable godknowswhere.

Have the laws of Science robbed us of mystery?
Is it all mindless, accidental chance?
Or a consequence of laws of Physics?
Or a fortuitous coincidence?

Yet all the pieces like a jigsaw
Dovetail together in harmony
From the subtlety of the atom
To the deepest recesses of a galaxy.

A microworld intertwined, attuned,
To supernovae, stars and moons.
Planets blasted from ghostly neutrinos,
Atomic micros to stupendous macros.

The trillion electrons in your eye
Are the same as in Eta Carinae,
Energies measured to sterling precision
Everywhere, without variation.

Throughout this common cosmography
We find exact uniformity.
A Universe expanding at the same rate
In every direction and in every place.

The Solar System seems too contrived
To have grown from laws and forces blind.
No. The orchestral cosmos sings
Under the baton of a Virtuosic King.

The way Pythagoras would have you hear
The silent Music of the Spheres,
Or a music hidden in silences we hear intuitively.
The marvellous, the majesty of a Universe's subtlety.

Evolution, biology can have their say.
We are here. Ah. Lucky me!
Perfect conditions for me to be.
Coincidences? Ratios? Simplicity?

Coincidences you cannot quantify.
Ratios between masses, energies,
Mathematical marvels,
Photons flitting electrically,

Forces unity, vivid complexities,
Facets of a Universe's simplicity
With the Baton of Teleology
Conducting the cosmology.

The Ultimate Mathematician,
The construct, a numerical Abstraction.
Between the laws of physics, maths,
Lies an astonishing Concordance,

And linked with reality, they dovetail
To a serene and deeper Resonance
That underlies our Creator, Mathematical,
True, alive, artistic and Eternal Consciousness.

MYSTERY NUMBER FIVE GRAVITY AND ELECTROMAGNETISM

"I was sitting in a chair in the patent office at Bern when all of a sudden a thought occurred to me: If a person falls freely he will not feel his own weight. I was startled."
Albert Einstein

The Gravitational Field
> May the force be strong! This one is weak.
> It had to be weak so we could exist.
> It takes all the weight of colossal Earth
> To pull an apple from a tree,
>
> Or drag a six-cornered snowflake down,
> Softly, tranquilly, to the ground.
> A bundle of atoms will hold the stem
> Of a cox's pippin on the bough
>
> Or a cherry as sunlight sweetens its heart,
> While the gravitational power of Earth
> Strains all the sunny, summer long
> To sunder the tree and fruit apart.
>
> Gravity attraction is weak.
> But cumulative, self-amplifying.
> Where matter is, it too is there,
> Deep in the heart of everywhere.
>
> If gravity were a more potent force
> In luminescent stars,
> Where heat radiating at the surface

Create an insufferable maelstrom,
Rife with photons carrying energy,
Then stars would burn faster, faster,
And so die younger, younger,
Too young in time for life to arrive,
Too young for intelligent life.
There would be no time for us.

If gravity were weaker
In luminescent stars,
Heat convective,
Gasses rising to the surface
Burning outwards into space
Would mean no supernovae,
No star formation nebulae.
Our Earth no bio-friendly place.

The Electromagnetic Field
Electrical attraction is strong.
Protons and electrons,
Plusses cancel minuses, self-limiting.
The forces between charged particles.
The ratio between the pair,
Electromagnetism and gravity,
Is a ratio extraordinaire.
One to ten to the power of forty.

If electromagnetism were stronger
The electric repulsion
Between protons would be greater.
No nuclear stability.
What in God's name would be our fate?

Electromagnetism and gravity are
Massively contrasting actualities.
That's the beauty of a Benign Electrician
To make them both just right.

Remember poor Goldilocks' enigma?
Mammy Bear's porridge too, too hot.
Daddy Bear's porridge too, too cold.
Baby Bear's porridge bowl right, just right.

We live in a well ordered cosmic expanse
With all the conditions conducive to life.
Remind me that all of this happened by chance!
With no Creative Significance!

MYSTERY NUMBER SIX THE CRITICAL DENSITY OF MATTER

"A lot of cosmic energy is embodied in the 3 kilos of matter in a new-born baby. A hurricane would have to rage for an hour to match it, or a large power station, to run for a year."
Nigel Calder

"Attractive gravity amplifies any deviation from the critical matter/ energy density, the repulsive gravity reduces any deviation from the critical density."
Brian Greene

Equations of General Relativity
Describe space and time, matter and gravity.
They opened the door to expanding space
With room for the cosmological trace.

Night sky pockmarked with pinpricks,
Astronomical photographs,
Look at the sky and what do you see
Smudges of clusters of galaxies

Rotating at tremendous speeds,
Swarming through billions of light years,
In darkness' and light's unforgiving seas,
Cycles of creating and recreating.

Clusters in clusters that infiltrate,
Intersperse, create and annihilate.
And there's billions more that we can't see.
All ripples in a seemingly pacific sea.

The balance between gravity
And matter's swelling run,
In a Universe, spatially flat,
Works if the critical density is one.

If more than one,
        Gravity would win
        And collapse all matter in a Big Crunch.

If less than one,
        Into thinner and thinner,
                Where expansion would be the outright winner.

But all the laws of Nature prove
That the critical density is point two seven.
The Density Designer hatching a heresy?
Or a figure that was made in Heaven?

Cosmologists knew there was something wrong.
Where was all the missing mass?
All that is visible to you and me
Is but four per cent of the density.

The rest of matter known to exist,
From the way that all the galaxies twist,
Dark Matter is known to be twenty-three.
Dark Energy is seventy-three.

Hubble, in the Roaring Twenties, found
Cosmic stretching was not slowing down?
The whole caboodle was speeding up?
Speeding from repulsive gravity?

The Cosmological Energy
That infiltrates every nook and cranny
Fitted the jigsaw beautifully.
God only knows what this could be!

It instilled a springiness to space,
And put attractive gravity in its place.
Without it, gravity would be king,
As it was in the beginning.

More, more space to hold less matter,
As fuel was added to the flames,
As all spacetime was expanding
The density of matter waned, waned,

Diluting, stretching, fissioning.
At some point in the rigmarole,
A couple of billion years ago,
Dark Energy forces took control

With the power of repulsive gravity.
Repulsion greater than attraction,
To dominate the speeding up
At the end of galaxy formation.

Distant galaxies, supernovae,
Rushing away like flotsam adrift,
The farther, the faster, and measured by
The stretching light-waves--- red shift.

With the advent of inflation
In the opening seconds of creation,
Irregularities infinitesimally small,
One part in a hundred thousand parts,

Were just the right size for life to commence.
These were the seeds of galaxies,
Of all the planets and stars that be,
Of intelligent observers, you and me.

This quintessence added on
To elements, Dark Matter, neutrinos, photons,
A new Theory of Aligned Symmetries.
Safe to say we know little of it.

What strange Coincidence triggered this?
Who turned this energy in a way
It has had the right aptitude today
Compared to other densities?

But some Revelation will let us know
When the Grand Designer determines so.
Imprinted fingerprints at the start,
Reflect the kindness in the Creator's heart.

The Chemist who predesigned this figure
Understood the bigger picture.
Another cosmic coincidence,
A masterpiece of divine Omniscience,

Made by a Divine Intelligence.
For us who only stand and stare
Where lives a physicist with stars in her eyes
Who's dying to win the Nobel Prize?

In these days when galaxies dominate,
If it were bigger we would not lie
Around to wonder why we wonder
Or wonder why we wonder why.

MYSTERY NUMBER SEVEN SUPERSYMETRINOS

"Nature abhors a vacuum."
Benedict Spinoza
"Twas brillig and the slithy toves
Did gyre and gimble in the wabe;

All mimsy were the borogoves
And the mome raths outgrabe."
Lewis Carroll

Whence came all these Immutable laws?
To forge, to conceive, to contrive and to weave?
Are they the constructs we can't see
Of more fundamental energies?

Can particles each have super partners
All unified in Supersymmetry?
Could it be a quark has a partner squark?
A lepton have a slepton?

An electron have a selectron?
A neutrino have a sneutrino?
A photon have a photino?
A graviton a gravitino?

A Higgs bosun a Higgsino?
And all those particlinos
Unmeasureable and unseeno?
What language do you think they are writtenino?

What other scenariosinos
Could possibly sexist?
Could this be a true sinterpretation
Of our simple Mother Natureino?

What of sDark Matter, sDark Energy,
Have they superpartnerinos?
Are the physicists out on a brambleino
Needing to drill where the wood is sthick?

We are left with sparticles and forceinos,
Sforces and particleinos
And whateverino
You sthink yourself.

What Somnicient Divinityino
Could create such scenariosinos?
And sincludeino the sprospectus
Such sexiguities in the designino?

MYSTERY NUMBER EIGHT STRING THEORY

*"The particle-as-dot model is an approximation of a more refined
portrayal in which each particle is a tiny vibrating filament of energy,
called a string. Yet because they are so small, some hundred, billion,
billion times smaller than one atomic nucleus, they appear as points."*
Brian Greene

Perhaps the point-like vibrating Strings,
The latest inkling on the nature of things
Are vibrations along a stretch of things.
A Theory with twenty-five dimensions,
A particle faster than the light,
Particles that can find no rest,
Without fermions, without quarks.

Lo! A new Superstring Theory,
Consistent with Quantum and Relativity.
Vibrating, oscillating, dancing loops,
Particles vibrating harmonic notes,
Resonances determining mass and force,

In unified deepest Harmonies:
Reflections of an Absolute Consciousness.

Each string of energy which is Eternal,
The musical dance of the fundamentals,
Choreographed by physics rules,
The foundation of our understanding
Of the beauty of the wonders there,
A richly-twirling labyrinth veiled in mystery
Twisting and unfurling rhythmically.

Dazzling! Exhilarating!
Strings that quiver and kiss and hoop,
Into a photon, a closed string loop.
Never still. Dashing at light speed.
Here all fundamental particles unite
And all the forces are unified.
Force and motion come together
As vibrations on these minikin strings.

Really, field lines are what exist.
Strings' field lines of electric flux,
Forces field lines that stretch between.
Fundamental, Beautiful and Serene.
All the bosons, all the fermions,
Laws of forces, particle motions
Are seen as String Oscillations.

In the 1920s Theodor Kalusa
Applied the mathematics of waves to atoms,
To unify gravity and electromagnetics.

Fundamental particles became vibrations
And differences became harmonics
So the universe is all Musical tones.
This M-theory. Is it Membrane, Music
Or an unMeasurable Mystery?

John Schultz began this revolution.
Then received his deserved promotion.
But problems arose in the geometries
Of unseen dimensions that needed solutions;
Instabilities in constants and equations;
Predictions ending in infinite versions?
Oh! It may be right but it can't be proved!

There always will be alternative views!
And M-theory, unique and all-embracing,
Is conjecture that masquerades as fact
With the possibility all may be wrong.
No principles! No precise equations!
Perhaps lost in the physics' sociology,
Physicists can't see the wood for the trees!

Or physicists, maybe, are deluded
By the astounding significance
Of their own innate intuitions,
That arise outside their own volition,
The meanings behind personal evidence
While deeply trying to comprehend
The mystery of all that we do and don't understand.

Perhaps they inadvertently ignore
The enigmatic Consciousness,
The miraculous Transcendence
Of love, ideals, intellect, faith, sanctity,
The invisible, mystical side of things,
Its divine and its human reality,
And the wonder of all life's mysteries.

This is when the Spirit sense
Hold an affinity with the Divine,
That guides us on towards intuitive faith
In a numinous, non-empirical state,
Towards awe, sanctity and revelation,
The beauty of supernatural causation,
That springs from our being alive, our Consciousness.

The landscape of String is unseeable.
This grand unification of particles, forces,
Of Quantum and Relativity,
With Dark Matter, Dark Energy,
Still a web of conjecture, ambiguity,
A belvedere of a deepening mystery,
Like winks in the Creator's eye.

MYSTERY NUMBER NINE UNPREDICTABILITY

*"The artist appeals to that part of our being which is more
permanently enduring. He speaks to our capacity for delight and
wonder, to the sense of mystery surrounding
our lives: to our sense of pity, and beauty, and pain."*
Joseph Conrad

All things are marvellous and mysterious.
Do not take anything for granted.
They may or may not be the ultimate field.
These are the things we know and think on
To reveal every natural phenomenon
In the Earth, the Stars, the Rain, the Snow
And all we think we need to know.

So from here where do we think we go?
We go to the place we think we know.
Who knows? Be assured no one is sure.
The past and present engender the future
And the future is a child of the past.
We have come a long way and now we know
We have a very, very, long way to go.

And the little electrons still danced and spun
Near the speed of light, they would prance and turn
In a quantum dance of perpetual fun,
All enmeshed and interconnected
Within a creative Consciousness,
With conscious energy, waves, excitations
Moving through all in collective vibrations.

All this quantum uncertainty reflects
Miles of unpredictability,
In the weather, thunderstorms, ocean waves,
Auroras, waterfalls, discoteque raves,
In the Earth's gargantuan gravity
That all summer drags a cherry down a tree,
In volcanoes, red sunsets, light rain-bowed apart,

In star-bursts, pulsars, supernovae
Along the spectrum of which we are part
To the indeterminacy of the human heart.
Years of physics research have found
Sub-nuclear, elegant interactions abound,
So many overlapping fields,
Broken and unbroken symmetries.

Particles in nanotechnology
Move in perpetual symmetry.
And space teems with popping transients.
Electromagnetic photons chase
Across the corrugations of space,
And the w's and z's of the weak force
Absorb the Higgs, those eerie ghosts.

Yet all is no more than a glimpse of Creation.
Whatever reality is spawned in time,
The quantum theory stands sublime,
And micro-fundamental indivisibles,
Cradling real, imaginary particles,
That show profound, unanswered possibilities,
Take us to the edge of the mysteries.

What astonishing Intellectuality
Could hoard such incredible depositories,
These cosmological, infinite treasuries,
Those invisible, mirror-image tapestries?
We have but little hope to one day draw
A beautiful, unified, ultimate Law.

A Theory of All-There-Is
That exists
Enmeshed
Within the Ineffable Consciousness?

MYSTERY NUMBER TEN A THEORY OF CONSCIOUSNESS (TOC)

"I can answer in two words, im- possible."
Sam Goldwyn
"Mathematics is the science of the infinite."
Hermann Weyl

Is it possible a simple,
Singular verse
Could explain the workings
Of the Universe?

Einstein was certain
There must be
Since all had one,
Singular infancy.

As it was in the beginning...
In that Singularity...
All matter;
Its emanation gravity;
Magnetism;
Electricity;
The strong and the weak nuclear forces;
Radio waves;
Light;
Gamma ray sources;
Time's ever-changing velocities;
Space's never-ending curvatures;
With both in Spacetime,
Integrally wrapped
In a singular, continuous manifold
Of inconceivable energies;
Awash with waves in all directions;
Electrons;
Photons;
Gravitons;
Protons;
Fields outspread across space and time;
Mass;
Motion;
Speed;
acceleration;
And the all-pervasive Consciousness.
Consciousness is eternal.

All of these once had a shared existence...
All of these share equivalence.

All of these are interchangeable
At a defined rate of exchange,
For nothing is lost,
Nothing is gained
In every energy exchange;
Nothing is gained,
Nothing is lost
In every nuclear holocaust.
Energy is eternal.

Light is the secret of all that exists…
Without it,
All we know could not be,
A quantum cascade pure and simple,
Made of energy photons,
So, so, so small
On the brink of being invisible!
But they gather,
Accumulate
And feature
As a dominant force of nature.
Light is eternal.

Subatomic particles are energy too…
Minute, potential
Transients
That pop in and out of virtual existence,
In millionths of a second
Filling vacuums
With hypotheticals,
Awaiting alternative possibilities,

Fields flashing simultaneously.
Energy is eternal.

All cutting capers of joviality…
All interconnected,
Interpenetrating
Potentials that may become actuals,
All partners in a continuous,
Tumultuous
Dance of Creation,
Of annihilation,
Of transformation,
Of instantaneous interaction,
All eternally Longing-To-Be.
Dance is eternal.

All-embracing Consciousness…
Still it could be that this reality
Has just one fundamental entity?
A single Principle
To unify All?
One tapestry where all jigsaw pieces fall?
That embraces
And encompasses All?
Ah. Methinks there is one solution.
Consciousness encompasses All.
Consciousness is eternal.

MYSTERY NUMBER ELEVEN GRAVITY... THE SEARCH GOES ON...

"You and I are exceptions to the laws of nature; you have risen by your
gravity,
and I have sunk by my levity."
Sydney Smith

Gravity grazes a field on its own
But what was the nature of this creature?

To find its inherent qualities
Brilliant, tragic, Bronstien sought and tried,
As did Solomon before he too died.
Victims of Russian, German insanity!
Then de Witt found quantum gravity!
Bernstien went inside a black hole
And found that it had entropy
Proportional to horizon area.

Hawking showed it had temperature
And despite all the gobbled fuel,
Would cool! Imagine, cool?
Its heat will radiate until all
Its monstrous mass shrinks to a small
Singularity squeezed in by supergravity!

In the nutshell of supersymmetry.
There are problems with infinities,
Black hole densities, magnetic fields, gravities,
Infinite fluctuations, probabilities,
Such a variety of particles,

So many Constants, variables, incalculables.

The little electron's life depends
On paradoxes that never end,
While in infinite deeps of outer space
Mysteries deepen in the seen, the unseen.
Deepdownthings we know there's more
To comprehending the Real and the Unreal.

Missing links. An incomplete tale.
There are secrets Time may or will reveal.
We evolved from nothing
To something unbelievably real.
From real to something wonderful.
Mystical. Unknowable.

We are part of this Universe,
The matter that contemplates itself.
Nature is unforgiving to those
Who cannot prove what they propose.
The human intellect uses Nature's clues
To understand universal Truth.

The sweetest apple is nearest the Sun,
But reality is a fugitive on the run.
But Oh! The climbing will be such fun!
Our expectations second to none!
We await an Envoy to draw the veil.
A Magician to reveal the indivisible.

We live this side a stained-glass pane,

Glimpsing the Absolute Consciousness.
We see the cracks through which the light
Of the Ineffable comes into sight.
Cracks through which enlightenments appear
That draw the aureoled Marvellous near.

All the while in the brightening sunlight
With wild varieties of every hue,
Of reds, of greens, of whites, of blues,
We roam a mystical Universe
Pixillated with mysteries, wonders,
That same Ineffable Creator made.

Still the search goes on. We wonder why
We wonder why we wonder…
A physicists' solution there yet might be.
Who knows what the missing links may be?
What that grand Principle might be
When Quantum lies down with Relativity?

Along the winding rooms of unknowing,
Scientists measure mere certainty.
We have no need for certainties,
We have no need for absolutes,
And the essence of knowledge
Will always flounder, happily, in doubts?

Chapter Nineteen

The Spectrum of Consciousness at the Heart of the Matter

UNIT ONE HUMAN CONSCIOUSNESS

"No philosopher or novelist has ever managed to explain what that weird stuff,
human consciousness, is really made of…"
Iris Murdoch

"Within thirty years, we will have the technological means to create superhuman intelligence.
Shortly after, the human era will be ended…"
Vernor Vinge, 1993

The human brain is the dream machine.
Three pounds of tapioca-like goop.
With alpha waves oscillating
Ten times a second, startling.
Beta waves faster by three times,
Reflecting, concentrating reflexes.

One hundred billion neurons interacting
With about ten thousand more.
Electrical impulses via dendrites
Transmitting via axons to bridge the loops.
Nerve cell ends with specialised synapses
Turning electric signals to molecules.

Neurotransmitters triggering impulses;
Unconsciously processing and distilling
Sensory input in the here and now,
And all these together endow
The ineffable, mindful sense of self,
Our awesome Consciousness.

Our wrinkled cerebral cortex
Hides the convoluted Transcendence
In the buckling rucks of its surface.
It's accelerated evolution
Led to different morphologies.

Different cognitive capacities,
Intuitive aspects like mood and perception,
Emotion, memory and cognition,
Are far removed from genetic influence.
Yet beyond a world of joy and pain
There lies a real, Transcendent Domain.

Behind the veils of stars and sky
An unseen, mysterious reality
And it lies within our Consciousness.
There are layers of this Consciousness,

Hidden, enigmatic, of which we are aware
The same way the Sun's core is inaccessible

And yet we know what's there!
Or is that light on in the fridge?
Open the door and it is there!
The awareness of living infinity!

I can never predicate
What you might say or do,
Nor anticipate
Any of your changing thought,
Nor replicate
The gentle flappings

Of trillions of fritillaries
That constitute
Your Conscious Mind,
Nor your private thoughts compute.
You, a divine fragment of All-There-Is,
In life sharing all nuances of creation.

And you send out contact lines, intersecting
Other's thoughts on the psychic plane
Like millions of lights simultaneously
Criss-crossing the night sky.
And every fragment is cherished delicately
And known instantaneously

In an integrated response
For Consciousness is everywhere at once.

All the grand magnificence,
All the grand reality we share,
All the pulsating Consciousness,
Echoing within the vast Awareness

Cherishes the illusion of Separateness.
And our mind, mind creates, recreates,
And changes probabilities.
Wishes become real, desires fulfilled,
What we see become newer realities
In creation's spontaneous simultaneity.

All-There-Is speaks softly to us,
Wallows in our creativity
And faith leads us to wonder, fulfilment,
Full of sustenance and spontaneity
In our magical environment.

So we can smile at the Wholeness,
Rise above our powerlessness
Knowing our spirituality
Is one with all Conscious reality
And dance the joy of creativeness.

And Consciousness lies beyond science's grasp,
For atoms alone cannot conspire
To create thought, compassion, beauty, love's fire,
Prayer, hope, faith, morality,
Or the wonders of the heart's desire.

UNIT TWO A CONSCIOUS UNIVERSE

*"Mind no longer appears as an accidental intruder into the realm of
matter; We are beginning
to suspect that we ought rather to hail it as the Creator and Governor
of the realm of matter."*
James Jeans

*"The quest to understand the nature of matter and the Universe of
space and time may come to rely
uniquely and completely upon the beckoning or the avoidance of the
infinite.
We will need to know it better than we know ourselves."*
J. D. Barrow

A Conscious Universe?
Now there's a thought!
Its wholeness grounded in physics laws.
Trillions of creative interactions
Have many a tale to tell!
The infinitesimal and infinite gell
With precision, actual and spiritual,
In an Absolute Collective Unconscious.

This gives birth to every Consciousness,
Each level interpenetrating.
From the fundamental particle
To biological sentient life,
To wider, widening awakenings,
To greater reflective mindfulness,
To transcendent contemplations
Where the soul appreciates and perceives
A wider, discerning belvedere.

And life is the journey getting there.
Self-infused in the Absolute,
The Indefinable Consciousness.
Plants demonstrate intelligent behaviour.
A tiny shoot senses its competitor;
Leaves, seeds, flowers are aware
Of their purpose in being there;
Birds sing, sing a higher pitch
In a noisy, urban thoroughfare;
Animals and fish are aware.
Dogs obey their master's voice
And birds know more than we think.
Music is more than oscillating
Molecules of random air.

Homo sapiens has unimaginable possibilities
And all beginnings are ends,
All ends are, in a sense, beginnings,
Crucibles for creation, recreation,
Of our changing incarnations.
Consciousness rooted in
Electrical, chemical, physical properties,
That stretch way beyond genetics
To newer, Transcendent Realities.

This Spectrum of Consciousness
Is an ocean of Mystical Light,
Always beyond the physics
Which studies the material,
Not unlike electromagnetics,
With inseparable interconnectedness,

Interpenetrating seamlessly,
Adjusting, readjusting endlessly,
Accommodating all life inexplicably.

A cosmic, Collective Consciousness,
From the material to the luminous,
From the elementary particle
To the mystical transcendent spirit
Enfolding All-There-Is holistically
Like water enwraps innumerable fish,
And unfolds, enfolds and unfolds,
Explicating the implicate order
To shape the patterns of matter.

Serendipitously, it came to pass,
The Quantum, Consciousness interface.
Searching for noisy, poltergeist spooks
That shifted furniture around a room,
Dick Bierman found strange noises came
During a Champions League football match,
Atletico Madrid versus Ajax.
The high point was the Ajax goal.
The only score in the game!
And later replicated in New York Towers!

Perhaps our Collective Consciousness
Sprung from global randomness
Is keeping the Universe in its place
That created it in the first place,
Spawned by a Grand Divine Designer.
Stranger than fiction, quantum is.

The observer decides how a particle is.
Observe a blossoming chestnut tree.
Looking changes the particles' states.
There's no tree unless you look to see!
We are observers, participants
In the here-and-now scenario,
In the faraway, in the long ago
As particles commune in every place,
Transcending boundaries of time and space.

Humanity hardwired to its gladness,
To the holistic divinity within
That mirrors us, mirroring Him.
The particle, wave duality
Transforming doubt into certainty,
Photons bilocating, interfering all the time.

Consciousness that endows the flowering
Of gentle prevalence, vitality, fertility,
In quantum transformations
Under clouds of probability,
In molecules perfectly attuned to sing
Like pearls along a necklace string,
In atomic loops of creativity
That metamorphose from primal things
Into meditative, intelligent beings.

Intelligent life a necessity
For the Universe to have reality.
Genesis created because we see.
No Universe could come to be

Unless Life, Consciousness, Seeing-to-See,
Had a guaranteed place in its history-to-be.
All evidence of Consciousness.

All the subatomic particles there are,
Will never tell us who we are.
Shaking a chalice of animate cells
Won't chisel a Michaelangelo:
Nor a repertoire of random sounds
Inspire a Brahms concerto:
Nor fingers on typewriters banging away
Shall not compare thee to a summer's day:
Nor a mountain of stones, none the same,
Won't on their own, make Notre Dame.

Intelligence, ordered by Consciousness,
Evolves what's to be or not to be.
The cosmos, a corner in God's eye,
Is driven by Spirituality.
None more so than mystics in meditation
Whose altered state of Consciousness,
Aligns with and enters the Wholeness,
Searching the mental Transcendental.

That is wholly immemorial
Sprung from the unknowable Divine,
Whole, indivisible, impossible to define,
Longings for the essence of that Consciousness
Attuned to the Collective Unconscious,
Longings to be one with and to sing
In the ocean from which the Eternal springs.

The ocean of Mystical Light lets fall
Energy that flows and permeates all.
This changing, evolves into matter
In a succession of instantaneous states,
Blinking in/out at incredible rates
Along that spectrum of Consciousness
Into endless patterns of orderliness,
Complexity beyond our conscious knowing.

And then we die and are not there
But our existence continues elsewhere.
In a timeless projection we take flight
To that vast ocean of mystical light.
Matter has wave and particulate aspects
When unobserved
And particulate ones when observed.
So, the idea that the observer
Creates everyday reality
Means his Consciousness is
A necessary ingredient
In the making/remaking of the universe.

The cosmos is a living organism
Crawling slowly, as the scientists see.
And all the journeys we trod, we trod,
Are seeing, knowing the Mind of God
Which breathes like a mystical open door
And is closer than ever imagined before.

Nothing is impossible to immortal You,
Communing Diamond in all you do,

Nearer to me than I am to me,
Efflorescences flowing from what is true.
A Consciousness that breathes
Of green things and the ineffable blue,
And arguments we can never be proved true.
And all that we know of all Creation,
May yet be subsumed in new revelations.
Some new evolutionary mystery,
As yet undreamt of in human philosophy.

Or is man fretted in greens and blues
On a blind trajectory he did not choose?
In fusions of traditions, of histories,
Of misunderstandings and mysteries
While all his unfinished work must ended be
At the horizon beyond which he cannot see
Where lies a deeper meaning, he must hope,
That breathes forever beyond his scope?

Who can tell who or when Time will reveal
Unique Designer calculations?
Here's to who will the future reveal
The discerning, Promethean blazes steal.

Chapter Twenty

The Heart of the Matter

UNIT ONE ENTANGLEMENT, ACROSS THE SOLITUDE OF LONELY SPACE

"Something that happens over here can be entwined with something that happens over there even if nothing travels from here to there—and even if there isn't enough time for anything, even light, to travel between the events."
Brian Greene

In a cosmos communing
Instantaneously,
Two photons emitted from one source,
Simultaneously communicate
Faster than the speed of light,
Across the solitude of lonely space.

Antithetical twin particles. One can dance
In curling loops, in lunular hoops,
Anguilline postules, orbicular scoops.
The other similar but in reverse.
Both locked in a passionate embrace
Across the solitude of lonely space.

Quantum mechanics always ensures
Entangled particles are never marooned,
But forever plugged into quantum rules,
All locked in a binding pact
No matter how near or far apart
Across the solitude of lonely space.

The paradox of paradoxes.
Not one is alone. But how can they know
What lies behind their deepest veils?
A ghostly brotherhood of ungraspables!
And inherently unpredictable!
Across the solitude of lonely space.

All in cosmic Connectedness
Outside time and outside space.
Schrodinger constructed the equation.
Electrons generate abstract wave functions
Inside uncertainty vibrations
Across the solitude of lonely space.

In complex relativity the Wave Function
Is the mental aspect of the electron
And it reacts to a quantum field

As you do to a situation!
So it is alive! Playing quantum games,
Across the solitude of lonely space.

It awakens the needs of the human soul
That lies at the heart of the unseen.
Our intelligent intent is available
To all gestalts of energy, immediately,
And through a process of cooperation
Thought is metamorphosed into action
Across the solitude of lonely space.

In phase entanglement, nerve cells there,
Instantaneously affect others elsewhere,
And quantum essences are aware,
Elusive, mysterious but everywhere.
At death, quantum information
Distributes into the Universe at large
Across the solitude of lonely space.

Some conscious states correlate
With particular regions of the brain.
But can we create a conscious state
By reassembling the atoms again?
In death the soul exists, subsists,
Wired to the Universal Soul
Across the solitude of lonely space.

The cosmos a seething shemozzle
Of rippling vacuum particles.
Oh! Oh! Oh! The senses boggle!

Popping in and out of existence!
A Universe still in a pure quantum state
Entangled as it was in the beginning,
Across the solitude of lonely space.

Where is an electron? We only know
Its probability when observed.
So, an electron wave spreading out
Does not exist in spacetime.
When electrons interact, they absorb or extract
A quantum of energy—light--
Across the solitude of lonely space,

Each leaves a remembrance
In the others heart
Which they can instantaneously enact.
So, every electron knows
Where every other electron is at!
Incomprehensible but a matter of fact
Across he solitude of lonely space.

When one electron blows his nose
Every other one jiggles his toes!
The principle of life is encoded
In beautiful quantum rules,
Sharing telepathic communion,
Here and there, once for all time
Across the solitude of lonely space.

Even particles understand and know
Because the cosmos is within us,

Where we came from and the return bus.
All part of a single Consciousness.
We are the way the cosmos conducts
Impromptu symphonic cadences
Across the solitude of lonely space.

UNIT TWO THE QUANTUM WAVE FUNCTION COLLAPSE, THE QUANTUM POTENTIAL: A VAST OCEAN OF MYSTICAL LIGHT

"'All energy contains consciousness.' That one sentence is basically scientific heresy, and in many circles, it is religious heresy as well. A recognition of that simple sentence would indeed change your world..."
Jane Roberts

Classical Physics tell you how, Quantum why.
In Spacetime we are the audience
Watching the drama unfold.
In Quantum, possibilities coexist
Until the observer looks to behold
The vast ocean of mystical light.

Every time we look to see
We perform the extraordinary.
Trigger the Collapse of the Wave Function,
The elusive domain of the Potential,
And create energy materialisation
From a vast ocean of mystical light.

The Quantum Potential is the timeless order,
Nature's self-organising principle.
Its creative power orders and complexifies,
Reaching out of uncertainties
Towards a more illumined clarity,
From a vast ocean of mystical light.

The irrepressible order of the world we breathe
Where molecules act Collectively
And the barrier between life, nonlife,
Evaporates into thin air
Because non-life material too is alive!
In the vast ocean of mystical light.

Ride a light beam. Time is still.
The quantum is superliminal.
An eternity of light that sometimes will
Freeze into matter so we and ours
Are light essences ultimately
Out of a vast ocean of mystical light.

Light is a particle, light is a wave.
The act of measuring obliterates
The wave, so light, the particle,
Becomes our objective reality.
And all seems incomprehensible
In a vast ocean of mystical light.

Its reality waves are not our reality.
Looking draws out the incredible
Creation of life's miracle.

It is metaphysical, mystical,
Interconnected, unpredictable,
From that vast ocean of mystical light.

Each elusive Possibility
Coexists simultaneously
In the enigmatic Wave Function
Where elementary particles behave
As either particles or waves
In a vast ocean of mystical light.

Don't look now, each electron is a wave!
Looking makes it a particle!
Forces the Wave Function to collapse.
Down there the quantum reality is unreal,
And its behaviour is surreal
In the vast ocean of mystical light.

Each with a Probability
To exist in the world we see,
Infinite choices in a timeless braid,
A web that reverberates everywhere.
All-That-There-Is, is Whole, is One,
In a vast ocean of mystical light.

The universe is One organism.
Matter, energy, Consciousness
Move towards a common purpose,
Each aspect of reality fused through willingness
Within each of all the others
Out of a vast ocean of mystical light.

Science and spirituality aspects
Want to be merged in Awareness,
In the ever-enfolding Consciousness
As the universe deciphers its own Being,
Desiring to know its own Longing-To-Be
From the vast ocean of mystical light.

In Quantum, matter is one and the same
As knotted, frozen energy.
Electrons jumping continuously
Absorbing, radiating differences,
With instantaneous influences,
Out of a vast ocean of mystical light.

Energy in discrete quanta.
Photons discontinuous, unseen,
From one state to another will go,
Never crossing the space between,
Instantaneously entangled
In a vast ocean of mystical light.

Two particles interacting
Are forever instantaneously
Connected by a quantum bond,
Portions gifted each to each,
In hyperspace, mysterious, beyond,
In the vast ocean of mystical light.

Time and space indistinguishable
And overlap until unidentifiable.
Spacetime, a higher dimensional place

Created out of forces, particles,
Stretched and distorted by matter in space
In the vast ocean of mystical light.

Spacetime a Continuum, everywhere,
As space contracts and time adjusts.
We march along at the speed of light
While Consciousness
Touches base and makes us aware
Of the vast ocean of mystical light.

Energy comes and energy goes,
Quanta entering or leaving matter,
And a gentle balance is imposed
As the probability of radiation decreases
And the frequency, energy, increases
Out of the vast ocean of mystical light.

All sorts of Potential energy exists
For time is space, matter is energy
In the classical Theory of Relativity,
And particles are waves,
While waves are particles
In the vast ocean of mystical light.

In the elusive Domain of the Potential
Energy gives rise to matter,
Bumps in space that vary with time.
The underlying Potential wells up
Those hidden enriching realities
Out of a vast ocean of mystical light.

The flow of the Quantum Wave Function
Lives in a secret invisible place,
Of incomplete Potentialities,
So waves will guide the particles,
Waves of Probability
Drifting in mists of mystical light.

Why is a particle in a wave state?
Is reality incomplete?
No. Spacetime and the Wave Function
Are rich, beautiful, mysterious aspects
Created by our Consciousness
In a vast ocean of mystical light.

A Wholeness undivided and in tune
With the infinite Possibilities
Of existence and essence totalities,
And as the Wave Function is observed,
It makes viable actualities
In the vast ocean of mystical light.

And where are they before observation?
In a superposition of all possible states,
In the inexplicable wave state.
Between the idea and actuality
Dreams the Potential reality
From the vast ocean of mystical light.

Time is the sequence of real events from which
The Collapse of the Wave Function springs,
The evolution of Possibilities

Into one functional Reality,
That complex, imaginary time brings,
From the vast ocean of mystical light.

UNIT THREE SO MANY POSSIBILITIES, ONE REALITY

"Exclusiveness is a characteristic of recent riches, high society and the
skunk."
Austin O'Malley

If ever you go to a Quantum place—
Newtonian Certainties disappear—
All things meld—one Reality—Emily--
All tuned in one Totality—A singular Multiplicity-

Peer—Peer—an Omnipotent gaze—
What you see—Believe—though strange—
A Consciousness-driven reality—
Speak quantum Logic exclusively—

Before you Choose—when you are near—
A billion Possibilities appear—
Universes that stare you in the face—
Choose One—the singular choice to be—
Its Existence grounded in time and space.
(Amen)

So we all drift in the complex
Dimension of space called Time.
And if the mathematics of relativity
Whose dimensions are real and imaginary

Are right, as Albert Einstein claimed,
We all move at the speed of light!
For time and space are inseparable,
The speed of light his final frontier.

The Wave Function's Potential ensemble,
Evolves deterministically,
The Schrodinger Equation is its solution
Which over time describes its evolution.

The Wave Function has potential states
But only one is revealed we know.
Yet it underlies and permeates
All of the universe as it goes.

In every Sacramental moment,
Each quantum event is a Handshake
Between the past and future,
Complex, unobservable and awake.

The actual superliminal linking
Beyond our three-dimensional state,
Once enacted in the past
Becomes a single waveform state.

The quantum universe is a seamless Whole,
No matter how far apart things be,
Sharing Instantaneously
Waves unmediated, immediately,

Phase entangled Interconnections,
That no physical signal could connect
Yet Bell's mathematical theorem proves
The non-local reality is immersed in it.

In this inaccessible Reality,
Timeless enigmatic correlations,
Enfolded, interpenetrated,
Are unfolded through our perception.

And empty space, alive, filled with virtuals
That pop off and on in ephemeral time,
Particles enfolding in and out,
Clouds of possible Probables,

Endlessly intermeshed waves of energy,
Jumping in indivisible quanta,
Never passing in between
Like the flashing sequence on a shutter screen.

Everything intermeshed with everything,
The Wave Function moves faster than light.
As does the Tachyon in Complex Space,
A hypothetical particle that underlies Spacetime.

A ghost that keeps reappearing!
A mirror image of our particle,
Its velocity increases
With energy loss!

As it loses energy it faster goes,
As it gains energy it slows,
Until all its energy is gone!
At zero energy, speed is infinite.

Add energy, it slows to speed of light!
A sort of strange transcendent wraith!
Maybe complex space could underlie
The Spacetime where we live and die?

Does the speed of light split the difference
Between Spacetime and Consciousness?
And what collapses the Wave function?
And how is Probability actualised?

As particles come into being,
All burning in the heraclitan fire,
So all matter in the universe
Must in some sense be Conscious.

Is it Consciousness observing
Or is matter itself somehow Aware
And the act of observation
Changes the particle's psyche there?

Difficult to imagine but imagine
Each particle and all matter
Eternally making choices!
So observation is Creation.

All creatures great and small,
All matter, rocks, particles, all,
Are mental with a Consciousness!
That's all there is for now folks! That's all!

All things alive in many strange states,
Running and jumping,
Colliding and bumping,
Is it time they were given centre stage?

The complex Wave Function is mental!
Time for physics to explore
The unobservable, inaccessible,
Consciousness, the Soul.

How is the world made fully Real?
Each step a conscious intent.
Actions translated into thought.
Creation out of Consciousness!

The universe is Whole, indivisible,
Interconnections innumerable,
Phase entanglement for real,
Its light permeates, underlies the real.

The study of physics must become
The study of the human Soul.
A mishmash cacophony of tuning strings
Becoming the euphony of living things.

All taking shape through the hidden domain
Out of the power of Consciousness
From the Collapse of the Wave Function
That sweeps all thought into action.

We live our lives in spacetime
That unfolds from the surreal,
The hidden wave function domain,
Of infinite Possibilities.

Oh. The real world requires quantum
As the source of its constituents
As the quantum requires the real
To engender all its real events.

Chapter Twenty-One

All a Matter of Life and Death

UNIT ONE IN MY FATHER'S HOUSE...

"If I am asked why I believe in God, I answer that it is because I believe in myself, for I feel it impossible to believe in my own existence without believing in the existence of Him, who lives as a Personal, All-seeing, All-judging Being in my conscience."
John Henry Newman

"The hierarchic chain of consciousness has many levels: physical, biological, mental, subtle, radiant and then... the soul finds itself alone with its own feelings and begins to perceive the gigantic reality of its own knowing..."
Jane Roberts

In my Father's House, Room Number One
Is our world of physical realities,
Built around relativity
Where the speed of light defines locality
And is the secret of all we see.

In my Father's House, Room Number Two
Is the Wave Function, home of Possibilities,
To be observed by someone real,
Unfolding to our perception,
Implying participation.

Where does the Wave Function collapse?
In between Quantum and Consciousness.
And when we see one possible outcome
Where do all the others go?
Away to parallel universes? Ho Ho Ho!

Or some superspace? Nobody knows.
Matter and spacetime is all that we see,
Bobbing, bobbing ceaselessly
On a vast ocean of mystical energy,
Mysterious, hidden from our view,

Where thought gives birth to the real world,
Matter's an expression of that thought.
Matter and mind are equivalent.
And both laced with Consciousness.
Fragments of a Divine Transcendent.

The universe is the expression
Of the dynamism of the Wave Function.
A universe pulsating on and off
As positrons, electrons annihilate
Into photons of energy,

Or superluminal energies
Into the dreams of other realities
Or Dark Matter setting spiral galaxies
Spinning at other velocities,
Undetectable but real as real,

And with each collapse of the Wave Function
Realities adjust simultaneously.
In death the body ceases to be
But the Wave Function and Consciousness
Remain and continuously see to see.

In my Father's House, Room Number Three,
We will ramble the lanes of infinity
Where Consciousness materialises
In swathes of astonishing disguises
Ineffable, inexpressible,

And, as yet, incomprehensible,
Portals in the unbroken Totality,
Bundled in the Marvellous,
All linked up superluminally
And the symbols of our waking world,

The symbols of our dreams,
All plucked out of the deeper depths,
Out of the Immutable Radiance.
In This there is no darkness,
But oceans of knowledge, truth and love.

Matter is waves in those timeless oceans,
A turbulence over serenest deeps.
Consciousness is the mystery
Where in special relativity
Simultaneous events

Depend on the frame of reference.
But in quantum the observer's mind,
The eye, the measuring instrument,
Which we call Consciousness
Becomes the creator of events,

Out of potentiality,
Out of hypnotic dreaming,
Out of the unconsciousness mystical,
Out of spirituality,
To the real actuality

In one miraculous sweep
And at the end when light goes dim
It relights a new reality.
As quantum systems merge and flow,
Entangled phases say hello,

Instantaneously in tow,
Identities change, identities grow,
Into the illimitable selves we know,
And gells with the Consciousnesses that go
In one, whole, integrated flow

So we are all learning as we go
How to handle fire, to search for truth,

How to find freedom, bit by bit,
In our little world made into a sphere
So that His Love might encircle it.

Infinity exists at every point in space,
It keeps a ubiquitous presence.
There cannot be a place called "there"
Because the self-same infinite is "here".

Eternity exists at every point of time,
With an ever-abiding residence.
There cannot be a time called "when"
And timelessness means there is no "then".

All space is in each point of space.
All time is in the present "now".
The infinite eternal is alive
At every point in space and time.

Each point connection
Is instantaneous.
We know because
We are the universe.

UNIT TWO ASPECTS OF NOW, OF LIFE AND OF DEATH

"Moments of time come to life when they are illuminated by the power of Consciousness. The flowing sensation from one moment to the next arises from our conscious recognition of change in our thoughts, feelings and perceptions. It seems to unfold into a coherent story."
Brian Greene

NOW, from which there is no escape,
Is the single friendship one must make.
The sacramental present tense.
It is. It is all. Life is never not NOW.

Our oldest memories once lived there.
The future will be now when it comes.
There is no theory to explain why anything can be.
No principle contains the ultimate mystery.

Creation is the here and Now.
Where it was, where it will be,
Are shadows of the essence
Of Creation's sweet ontology.

The Universe is recreated
In every instant of time.
Magnetic fields twirl high and low,
Space and time and gravity flow,

Haemoglobin molecule chains
In millions embark and terminate,
Electrons forever on the go,
All slithering in perpetual flow.

We do not see the changing rocks,
The rings in a flourishing tree,
Or the always falling pane of glass,
More a composite selection box.

Every Now is a new birth.
A gathering, a *meithel,* incredible,
Subsuming all in the wonder
Of a little room of the Universe.

We see change in the garden's history.
Snowdrop, tulip, agapanthus,
Buddlei, rose and dahlia clusters,
From frosty January to November bluster,

Change the belvedere day by day,
Change their petals, leaves and hues,
And yet we see but a single view,
A single moment in a given day.

Appearances may seem permanent
Yet fill illusion's pyre,
Created by the laws that burn
In the heraclitean fire.

So, Time is a permanent Now.
All that we see or do not see
Are shadows of how we view the reality
Of Creation's mystery.

All nature, all life is in communion,
Aligned with the Intelligence,
In the joy of Being, the sacred space,
No matter what ripples may take place.

I am Now. I am life.
I am silence. I am stillness.
I am intelligence.
I am Consciousness.

All part of the Universe's essence
That pauses on its way to express itself
As a galaxy, a planet, a moon, a sun,
A snowdrop, a chaffinch or a person.

Beyond our mind is a deeper knowing.
A greater Power to subsume our essence,
So, mastery of life allows you, being less,
Become aligned to that Consciousness.

Truth is more than the mind can know.
Our fears, desires, resentments, conflicts,
What always being the victim inflicts,
The bells that anger or self-pity ring,

Wanting always what the future may bring,
Are fictions that offer a sense of self,
A prison whose bars are in your head,
All added up, make a little dash
Between your birthdate and date of death
On a lonely gravestone when you're dead.

UNIT THREE DEATH AND ETERNAL LIFE, THE WHOLE SHEBANG IS A MYSTERY!

"Ah, Sweet mystery of Life at last I've found thee…"
Nelson Eddy's song
"Endlessly, we hurry up and down corridors, meeting people, knocking on doors, conducting our investigations. But the ultimate success will never be ours. Nowhere in the castle of science is there a final exit to the absolute truth."
Rudy Rucker

The whole shebang is a mystery!
Best to accept what's thrown at your feet.
The unacceptable, whatever it be,
Is the source of Grace, the fount of Peace,
The Now, a realisation of what must be,
A realisation of what it is to be.

The whole shebang is a mystery!
All those possibilities
Or call them probabilities
Of other unknown existences
At the cutting edge of the world we see,
The Sun, the garden, the skies and the seas.

The whole shebang is a mystery!
In the mists of all we cannot see,
Chameleon energies in disguise,
Like Dark Matter or Dark Energy,
Are as real as quantum uncertainty,
As real as the future before it can be.

The whole shebang is a mystery!
As invisible flames that hide in the light,
As real as knowing the Consciousness
That softly controls All-That-There-Is,
All these possibilities
Live in speculative realities.

The whole shebang is a mystery!
A Reality that gave rise to matter,
To life, intelligence, transcendence,
That asks itself questions like why?
And why? And where? And what?
And when? And if? And whether?

The whole shebang is a mystery!
Questions our ancestors could not imagine,
But who can unveil this reality?
But who will tell us where it could be?
Or uncover the language that it speaks?
What is the destiny it seeks?

The whole shebang is a mystery!
A garden that seethes with bright life all day
Embraces rot, dead leaves, decay.
Out of the moulder new embryos leap
And metamorphose in the compost heap.
Life's death brings life, new and vernal.

The whole shebang is a mystery!
Life that is created is eternal.
Things end. And each end is a little death.

From the jaws of death, new life springs.
In daily dying to ourselves
We enter into transcendence.

The whole shebang is a mystery!
Death is life's most precious thing.
The natural stillness that peace brings.
So a single death can ride the crest
Of all the waves of Consciousness
In Communion with all other deaths
And there lies the Resurrection.

The whole shebang is a mystery!
In all our thoughts of death and loss,
Stands, in stillness, the rough-hewn Cross.
Symbol of impending death
Of suffering, helplessness, loving, loss,
Of surrender, hope and victory won.
"Not my will but Thine be done."

The whole shebang is a mystery!
All will be well. Cross over the line.
The Cross is the face of the Divine.
The mystery all must face is death,
As fundamental to a life as breath.
Alone with all existence
In the dying of the light.

The whole shebang is a mystery!
After the senses close their eyes
And the shutter clutters down,

The final cosmic curtain call,
At the end of days consciousness is all
In instantaneous resurrection,
Mystical, panoramic animation.

The whole shebang is a mystery!
All light dwindles to a dimensionless point,
The miraculous moment of life's demise.
There where there is no time, no space.
Only existence and The loving Grace.
My mother, my father suddenly, waiting,
With all the others in truth will be there.

The whole shebang is a mystery!
Oh! This is a lovely being to be.
No one could ever imagine such.
Touching, a child perpetually
Skirting the brows of eternity.
All like a hazy summer's sight
Where all the lights go out into
An infinite gathering of light.

The whole shebang is a mystery!
Another existence beyond one we know.
Eternal life in another presence,
No neurophysiological explanations,
No existential hallucinations,
No complex memory formations.
Only faith-filled expectations.

Chapter Twenty-Two

All a Matter of Life and Death

UNIT ONE THE HUMAN SOUL

"Lord, if there is a Lord, save my soul, if I have a soul."
Joseph Renan

"Contemplation is the highest expression of man's intellectual and spiritual life. It is that life itself, fully awake, fully active, fully aware that it is alive. It is spiritual wonder. It is spontaneous awe at the sacredness of life, of being. It is gratitude for life, for awareness and for being."
Thomas Merton

The brain's network follows physics' laws,
With its neurons, synapses, in their billions,
Dreams, thought processes, decisions,
Prayers, memories, indecisions,
Looping, feedback twirling,

Leading to unavoidable
Unpredictability,

All part of the clockwork
Predetermined and fixed?
In essence, no free will?

Yet probabilistic quantum rules,
And spiritual dimensions mean
This never can be true.
We should know, we should predict,
In principle, what we should think.

And there is Chaos Theory too,
Simple cause to complex effect,
Butterfly flappings that make a tornado,
An unexpected surprising ripple,
At once random and unpredictable!

Our choices made from Consciousness
Are embedded in Spacetime,
In a future that is unknowable.
Which one of the possibilities
Will future time play out?

Soul, Psyche, Consciousness,
Where have they come from at our birth?
Where will they go to at our death?
How does brute matter, living cells,
Become conscious or self-conscious?

Look at a painting. What do you see?
Your impression of a pastoral scene
Which can instantaneously change,

Like infinite stills in a movie scene,
Because interpretations change

With the pastiche tinctures of the artist's paint
Reflected in your conscious state.
And you can never freeze the brain
Nor unravel the paint nor unpaint the scene.

The soul is Consciousness, self-aware,
With patterns of extraordinary shape,
Burning mentalities that transform
In time to realities of love, of faith.

When you take out Mary on a date
You can pulse, pulse, pulse the rate
Your heartbeat is singing in the rain,
A glorious feeling, I'm happy again!

From the first stir, the stir of romance
To the end, the ending of the dance
The passage of slow time, slow time
And consciousnesses rhyme.

Can we be so aware? What cause is there?
We follow the invisible flow of Time
Like the fossils of the trilobites
Illustrate past geological times.

Or that wonderful day you took my hand,
"You are the sweetest boy in the land!"
Or go on. Go back to the Big Bang.
How much all has changed since Time began?

With fossil memories everywhere,
Russian dolls in dolls in dolls,
Along the timeline as we fare.
Knowledge informs the conscious mind

And the brain sifts the richness there.
Richness written in the rocks
That carry the historical freight,
The sheer creativity of life,

The miracle of our Conscious State.
Consciousness of conscious reflections
Move through our minds or stick like glue
And some thought- patterns flicker through.

These spread in cosmic wave formations
To umpteen places at any one time,
We see what we are prepared to see,
Probabilities, in a strange reality clime.

And conscious minds share with other minds
Ideas, symbols, transcendent insight,
And souls search the most profound depths
Of the one mystical, intrinsic life

And the essence of all Consciousness
Twists the key to the Ultimate Truth,
And its self-awareness engineers
One's sympathy for another's tears,

And a faith that endows and sublimates
Love's ineffable attributes.
Consciousness is all there is,
The burning flames of the Universe.

UNIT TWO THE COSMIC SOUL

"Age cannot wither her, nor custom stale Her infinite variety."
William Shakespeare
*"What I embody, the principle of life, cannot be destroyed. It is
written in the cosmic code, the order of the universe. As I continued
to fall (To his imagined death) in the dark void, embraced by the
vault of the heavens, I sang of the stars and made my peace with the
universe."*
Heinz Pagels

For the Universe too has its own soul,
Alive, creating, beautiful, whole,
In its exchanging, its transforming,
Transcendental role.

One great, electromagnetic field,
Co-terminous with the universe,
One totality, all-inclusive,
All matter coupling and crisscrossing,

Illimitable space encompassing,
Here, there, everywhere, at once.
A telepathic universe.
Look in the mirror. All is reverse!

And you in the mirror live, alas,
A billionth of a second in the past!
See yourself in that light ray
That bounces to eye, to brain, away!

You will arrive but you are gone!
Existence is a twinkling day!
Look at the skies. The stars you see
Not as they are but as they were.

A point in space is a point in time.
A universe, its centre everywhere,
And its circumference nowhere!
The place from whence it came in time.

So everything you think you see
Exists in the light of history.
A star, thousands of light years hence,
Is as was then, not in the present tense.

Out there, somewhere, certain things
Have happened, have not yet happened,
Or are still happening!
Life, the Designer Engineer,

Perpetuates itself and steers
All forwards towards a dimensional point.
A miraculous gathering of light
Where all potentialities

Become ultimate realities.
Infinite suspended animation
In mansions of self-awareness
Subsumed into Omniscience.

Reflections in its cosmic soul,
The Consciousness of consciousness,
Reveal incredible coincidences
Rooted in bubbles of the past,

Flickering now in uncertainty mists,
But in shadows of the future, foresee
What was, what is and what will be.
Unimaginable dimensions

That we can see or cannot see,
Will light up an energy field of dreams,
Of peace, understanding, faith and hope,
With love, the gracious host, the guest,
The presiding, eternal isotope.

And this storm-tossed voyage still unfolds
Recesses hidden deep down Nature's hold
And Heaven's Absolute Consciousness,
Call it God or Heaven or What-You-Will,

Filled with the all-knowing Presences
From which springs all existences
Whose energy is Whole, is One,
Is a Consciousness Continuum.

A spectrum of Infinite Consciousness
While each thing longs after its own truth,
Aware of what it longs to be, to become,
Through its own innate, imbued creativity

In this universe's sweet reality
That leaves us wondering, wondering…
O We wonder why we wonder why
We wonder why we wonder…

UNIT THREE HERE WE ARE ON PLANET EARTH

Here we are on Planet Earth,
Ordinary place in the suburbs.

We have pulled some strings
On the nature of things
But know little of what future millennia will bring,
Or the teasing mysteries that wonder brings,
Or where the Mystical begins,
Or where the Ineffable spirit sings,
Or beyond the physics, what physics brings.
But we know the joy curiosity brings.

Here we are on Planet Earth,
Where humanity bows in a humble place.

The holiest altar in all space,
Peering down the infinitesimal place,
Down the scrambled, complex recesses,

Undreamed-of primordial addresses,
Larger and smaller than we can chase.
Where most of it is, is anyone's guess,
Where Dark Matter and Dark Energy race,
Wonders yet to be addressed.

Here we are on Planet Earth,
A rendezvous more complex than we can know.

Since thirteen point seven billion years ago,
Myriads of fine-tuned mysteries grow.
Why oh! why does it bother to be?
How did laws of nature come to be?
Who or what could have dreamed this show?
An impartial, infallible Impresario!
Still, uncertainties, possibilities flow.
The more we understand the less we know!

Here we are on Planet Earth,
Searching the ghostly signposts.

Along infinite motorways we go,
Watching for miracles to unfold,
In the half light, in darkness, in shadow,
Through a thin veil fretted in blues and greens
Longing for the mystical, the unseen,
Where flowers are singing in colours never seen,
And all our dreams and hopes are blessed
In the One Iridescent Consciousness.

And as we wait we are wondering,
Wondering why we wonder why
We wonder why we wonder…

UNIT FOUR WONDERING ABOUT THE GREAT COSMIC WHY?

"Exegi monumentum aere perennius… Non omnis moriar."
Horace
"Readers, my mantle I bequeath among ye…"
Kings 11

When we find solutions and think ourselves wise
Nature throws up an exotic surprise.
When we change the immutable,
Comprehend the inscrutable,
Make our dreams a reality,

Bet our life on probability,
When we witness quantum tunnelling,
And Black Hole matter funnelling,
We have moved from darkness into the light
Of the miraculous, incarnate, cosmic sight.

Remember when you wonder why
Or wonder why you wonder,
The Mathematician has done the maths
On the iota, the marvellous, the absolute,
And never made a blunder.

The question, "Does a God exist?"
Or call It "Consciousness", "Energy", the "One",
Or any name you care to say!
Multiplied by eternal joy, the probability, It may,
Will make it more than an infinite payday!

The consequence if it does not, will be
That you lose nothing at all.
So wager, wager! Have a gamble!
Take the odds for you may win!
And if you win, you will win all!

And God does not play dice with the Universe!
Or so a wise man said.
These probabilities for what they're worth
Only exist inside your head.
Horseman, throw the dice, on life and on death.

If you still doubt the numbers,
Can't get them round your head,
Think what Julian of Norwich said,
"All manner of things will be well."
You'll find out when you're dead.

Faith, the ineffable, precious gift,
Is not always a given thing
To those who know they think they know
Or those who do know everything!
It may well be true that we will not be able

To prove the ultimate win or loss
But we can draw conclusions.
Would a Deity create a brute-force cosmos
Or more hospitable conditions?
At times, indeed we have been forced

To rearrange our planets of belief
Because new concepts spring out of the blue,
Activate suspensions of our disbelief
Till we realise the new views are true!
When I stroll around the woodland paths

Strewn with autumnal leaves,
Leaves that simulate life's track,
Green, yellow, beige, brown and black,
Listening to chirping birdsong,
Choral harmonies in the trees.

The beauty that I see and hear
Is immeasurable more or less
Emanating from the stillnesses
Of the all-pervading Consciousness.

Think how the delicate snowdrop bows
Before the frost, hard winds and snows,
Or how a windswept tree will bend
Before the unforgiving wind.

Perhaps it's time to bow your head
In generous humility.
How small your presence must appear
In the light of a tiny galaxy.

And yet how great He has made you
In the light of the quantum scene,
Halfway between a star and an atom.
That's more than Intelligence can fathom!

You, trillions of cells, that operate together,
You Oh You, a complex entity.
A hundred times the stars in a galaxy
No matter what the weather.

Forget the maths, forget the cells,
He has you figured out.
Your destiny is in His palm,
Your unique fingerprints.

His perfect, dependable calculations
Tabernacle Hope in the mystery,
With electromagnetic molecules,
Strong force, weak force and gravity.

Nothing happened by accident,
Nothing was left to chance.
With rhythm, poise and balance,
The Dancer enacted the dance,

In the everlasting romance
With each credible, cosmic coincidence.
And we know more of an atom's life
Than we know about our darling wife!

Why we search for simplicity,
Why we run from who we are.
Why the sweetness of the night
As we watch the snowing stars.

Why we reach into the depths of light,
Why we seek silences of the soul.
Why things have beginnings at all times
And always go where they must go.

Why nothing happens everywhere
And everything happens nowhere.
Why everything now has always been
As it was once, is now, will be.

We wonder where Mister Time began,
Where Mister Time will end.
We wonder what Time is, how it bends
And how in every place it ends.

Why we think we are going where we are.
Why we have been where we think we have been.
Why we think we have been where we have been.
Why we are who we think we are.

Why we think we are who we are.
Why we wonder where we are going.
Why we wonder who we think we are.
Where we think we're going.

Where we think we've been.

Why we think we know where we're going.
Why we think we know where we've been.
Who we are and where we have been.

We wonder why we wonder why
We wonder why we wonder...

The End

Lightning Source UK Ltd.
Milton Keynes UK
UKHW041015170119
335716UK00001B/24/P